CHAMPIONS OF FREEDOM

The Ludwig von Mises Lecture Series

CHAMPIONS OF FREEDOM
Volume 31

Economic Theories and Controversies

Richard M. Ebeling
Editor

Hillsdale College Press
Hillsdale, Michigan 49242

Hillsdale College Press

CHAMPIONS OF FREEDOM
The Ludwig von Mises Lecture Series—Volume 31
Economic Theories and Controversies

©2004 Hillsdale College Press, Hillsdale, Michigan 49242

First printing 2004

Printed in the United States of America

Front cover: © Images.com/CORBIS

Library of Congress Control Number 2003115098
ISBN 0-916308-52-9

Contents

Contributors

James M. Buchanan, winner of the 1986 Alfred Nobel Memorial Prize in Economic Sciences, is Distinguished Professor Emeritus of Economics at George Mason University and Distinguished Professor Emeritus of Economics and Philosophy at Virginia Polytechnic Institute and State University. He is best known for developing the "public choice theory" of economics, which changed the way economists analyze economic and political decisionmaking. Professor Buchanan received a B.A. from Middle Tennessee State College in 1940, an M.S. from the University of Tennessee in 1941, and a Ph.D. from the University of Chicago in 1948. He has taught at the University of Virginia and UCLA. Among his many books are *The Calculus of Consent: Logical Foundations of Constitutional Democracy*, with Gordon Tullock; *Cost and Choice; The Limits of Liberty; Liberty, Market, and State; Better than Plowing and Other Personal Essays*; and the 21-volume set, *The Collected Works of James M. Buchanan*.

William R. Dougan is Professor of Economics at Clemson University, where he currently serves as chairman of the John E. Walker Department of Economics. He has previously taught at Colgate University, Dartmouth College, and the University of Chicago's Graduate School of Business, and has served as a consultant to the Federal Trade Commission and the World Bank. Professor Dougan received his B.A. from the University of Virginia and his Ph.D. from the University of Chicago. His primary research interest is the economics of the public sector, but his publications also include articles on microeconomic theory, monetary economics, and psychological aspects of economic behavior.

Richard M. Ebeling is President of the Foundation for Economic Education (FEE) in Irvington-on-Hudson, New York, the oldest institution in the United States devoted to the philosophy of individual freedom. Prior to his appointment at FEE in May 2003, Dr. Ebeling was the Ludwig von Mises Professor of Economics (1988–2003) and Chairman of the Department of Economics and Business Administration at Hillsdale College. He also served as Vice-President of the Future of Freedom Foundation (1990–2003). He lectures extensively on a variety of economic and pulic policy topics throughout the United States, Latin America, Eastern Europe, and the former Soviet Union, where he has consulted with the Lithuanian government, the city of Moscow, and the Russian Parliament. His most recent book is *Austrian Economics and the Political Economy of Freedom* (Edward Elgar, 2003); his next book, *Monetary Central Planning and the State*, is scheduled for publication in 2004. He is the editor of the three-volume *Selected Writings of Ludwig von Mises*, which is based primarily on Mises' papers unearthed in a formerly secret Moscow archive; two volumes have been published by Liberty Fund of Indianapolis. He has edited fourteen volumes in the *Champion of Freedom* series from Hillsdale College Press, as well as several other works, including *The Dangers of Socialized Medicine* (1994), *The Case for Free Trade and Open Immigration* (1995), *The Failure of America's Foreign Wars* (1996), *The Tyranny of Gun Control* (1997), and *Liberty Security and the War on Terrorism* (2003). Dr. Ebeling is currently working on an intellectual biography of the Austrian economist Ludwig von Mises.

Nolan Finley is Editorial Page Editor of *The Detroit News*, where he also writes a Sunday column. Prior to that, Mr. Finley was the newspaper's Deputy Managing Editor, directing the newsroom. He has also served as Business Editor, and in various editing positions on the city, state, and metro desks. As a reporter, he covered Detroit City Hall during the Coleman Young administration. He has been with the newspaper for 27 years, starting as a copy boy in the newsroom while a student at Wayne State University. He is a graduate of both Schoolcraft College in Livonia and Wayne State, where he earned a B.A. in journalism.

George Gilder, Chairman of Gilder Publishing LLC, is a Senior Fellow at the Discovery Institute. Mr. Gilder attended Exeter Academy and Harvard University. While at Harvard, he studied under Henry Kissinger and helped found *Advance*, a journal of political thought. He was later a fellow at the Kennedy Institute of Politics and editor of the *Ripon Forum*. He has served as a speechwriter for Nelson Rockefeller, George Romney, and Richard Nixon, among others. He is the author of several books, including *Men and Marriage, Visible Man, Wealth and Poverty, The Spirit of Enterprise, Microcosm*, and *Telecosm*. A pioneer in the formulation of supply-side economics, he is a contributing editor of *Forbes* magazine and a frequent writer for *The Wall Street Journal* and other publications. A study of Ronald Reagan's speeches showed that Mr. Gilder was Reagan's most-quoted living author.

Charles L. Griswold, Jr., is Professor of Philosophy and Chairman of the Philosophy Department at Boston University. Dr. Griswold has also been Visiting Professor at Georgetown University and Olmsted Visiting Professor in Ethics at Yale University. He is the author of *Self Knowledge in Plato's Phaedrus*—which received the Franklin J. Matchette Prize from the American Philosophical Association—and *Adam Smith and the Virtues of Enlightenment*. He is also editor of *Platonic Writings, Platonic Readings*, and has published widely on the history of philosophy and on political thought. He is the recipient of awards and fellowships from the Earhart Foundation, the National Endowment for the Humanities, the National Humanities Center, and the Woodrow Wilson Center, among others. He is currently at work on articles on various topics, such as Platonic philosophy and the problem of moral realism. His next book will focus on the problem of reconciliation with imperfection.

Lucas E. Morel is Associate Professor of Politics at Washington and Lee University, where he teaches courses on American government, political philosophy, black American politics, Abraham Lincoln, and politics and literature. He is author of *Lincoln's Sacred Effort: Defining Religion's Role in American Self-Government* and editor of *Ralph Ellison and the Raft of Hope: A Political Companion to "Invisible Man."* Dr. Morel is a member of the Scholarly Advisory Committee to the Abraham Lincoln Bicentennial Commission. He has also written editorials for the

Los Angeles Times, Christian Science Monitor, and *Richmond Times-Dispatch,* and appeared as a commentator on CNN's *TalkBack Live* and Wisconsin, New Hampshire, and Virginia Public Radio. Dr. Morel holds a Ph.D. in political science from The Claremont Graduate School.

Joshua Muravchik, a resident scholar at the American Enterprise Institute and a specialist in U.S. foreign policy and international relations, received his Ph.D. in international relations from Georgetown University and his B.A. from City College of New York. Dr. Muravchik serves as an adjunct scholar at the Washington Institute on Near East Policy and is an adjunct professor at the Institute of World Politics. He is a member of the editorial boards of *World Affairs,* the *Journal of Democracy,* and *Orbis.* He has written extensively about the role of ideas and ideologies in international politics and his articles have appeared in numerous publications, including *Commentary,* the *New Republic,* the *New York Times, The Wall Street Journal,* the *Washington Post,* and the *New York Times Magazine.* He is the author of several books including *Exporting Democracy: Fulfilling America's Destiny* and *Heaven on Earth: The Rise and Fall of Socialism.*

Joseph A. Stanislaw, cofounder and President of Cambridge Energy Research Associates (CERA), holds a B.A. from Harvard University and a Ph.D. from Edinburgh University. Dr. Stanislaw has been a professor and lecturer in economics at Cambridge University, a member of the Energy Research Group in the University's Cavendish Laboratory, and subsequently, Senior Energy Economist at the International Energy Agency in Paris. He is an internationally recognized authority on energy markets, geopolitics, and corporate strategy. As CERA's president he oversees the company's global operations and directs its *Global Energy Watch,* a report on world energy economics and markets. He is co-author, with Daniel Yergin, of *The Commanding Heights: The Battle for the World Economy,* which examines the diminishing role of the state and the growing role of the marketplace and private enterprise in the world economy. The book has been praised by the *Los Angeles Times, The New York Times Book Review,* and *The Wall Street Journal.*

Foreword

This is the 31st volume in the Hillsdale College Press series Champions of Freedom. Compiled from the Ludwig von Mises Lecture series, which has been held for over three decades at the College, Champions of Freedom was begun under the presidency of George Roche III. George began his career at the Foundation for Economic Education where he became an admirer and a colleague of Ludwig von Mises.

Hillsdale College was built under the influence of the American Revolution. In that revolution there was much talk of property rights. These are rights, said Madison, to the material things that we have made and earned. These are also rights to every natural property that belongs to the human being. This means his ability to think and to speak. It means his capacity to worship the Almighty, and his individual responsibility to that highest Being. Property rights are a kind of summation of all of our rights.

In modern times, many great economists have worked to recover the full force of this powerful view, which has been the chief foundation of liberty in the modern world. Among these economists, none is more important than the great Ludwig von Mises.

This year, Hillsdale's long-time Ludwig von Mises Professor of Economics (and editor of this book series), Richard Ebeling, has moved on to become president of the Foundation for Economic Education. We wish him well, and look forward to continuing to work with him in the cause of liberty.

LARRY P. ARNN
President
Hillsdale College

Introduction

How often do we look at those around us and think how absurd, dangerous, misguided, or foolish is so much of their conduct? How often do we, then, think to ourselves: If only they would listen to what we have to say, do as we suggest, learn from our experiences, and act in ways that we know would be far better for them? And how often are we amazed that the vast majority of people wish to make up their own minds, follow their own best judgment, and choose their own ends to pursue and select the means they consider most appropriate?

One reason we so frequently have these thoughts and are frustrated by the actions of others is that each one of us is basically a central planner and a social engineer. Indeed, we cannot help being so. How else could we live our everyday lives if we did not plan our activities with the goal of engineering an outcome more to our liking than if we did nothing and let whatever comes determine our fate? Whether it is the profound things or the mundane, we are constantly planning and engineering.

Virtually all economists emphasize that choice and decisionmaking are inseparable from the human condition. There are things we want and we have to do things to get them. But the inevitable discovery that many of the means to our desired ends are scarce—that is, are not available to us in sufficient quantity and quality to attain all the ends for which they might be applied—imposes upon us the necessity of choice. We have to decide which among those desired ends we consider more important and which less important. In other words, we have to rank our desired ends in some order of importance so as to decide for which of these competing and desired purposes those scarce means will be applied, since some of those desired ends will have to go totally or partially unfulfilled. We also have to decide what are the acceptable trade-offs in life, in terms of what and how much we are willing to give up of one desired goal or purpose to be able to successfully obtain some amount of another.

In all of this, we are acting as the planner of our own lives. We select the ends worth pursuing, we decide on the use of the means, and we implement our "plan." We adjust our actions to fit the blueprints we have constructed in our own minds, because we understand that unless we make most of our actions conform to "the plan" we may fail in attaining those ends we have decided are the relatively most important. Of course, sometimes we "cheat" on our plan. We are lazy, thoughtless, undisciplined, and easily distracted by momentary pleasures and temptations that lure us away from all that may be necessary for the plan's achievement. We sometimes, therefore, act as "traitors" and "saboteurs" of our own plans. We become our own "subversives."

What we discover in the planning and engineering of our own lives is that there are multitudes of millions of other individual human planners. Each one is doing the same things we are: selecting among ends, deciding on the use of means, and setting various plans in motion. The question then arises, how shall we deal with these others, especially when their respective actions and use of various means under their control can very well influence the degree to which we are able to most fully attain the ends that we have decided to pursue?

There are basically only two alternatives: We can try to impose our plan on others and make all or some of their actions subservient to ours, or we can attempt to reconcile our plans with theirs by reaching some mutually agreeable terms of association. The first involves the use or the threat of some degree of force. The second involves peaceful, voluntary agreement.

The great danger from the use or the threat of coercion is not only that it denies freedom to those upon whom we use the force. That is certainly true, and in itself should raise moral objections to following this path. It denies to the individual who is coerced the right to make his own plans, design and engineer his own life, and have whatever degree of satisfaction that may come from the fact he has given his own meaning to his life. Thus, in various great things and small, the individual knows that for good or bad, successful or not, he has had a certain arena of his life in which he has been able to view himself as "the captain of his fate." To deprive a person of this liberty is to make him less than a full human being. It is to act, in a very fundamental sense, inhumanely.

But there is another great danger from the use of coercion or its threat. That danger comes from the fact that it can work. Slavery and serfdom have been among the most enduring social institutions throughout human history. Others can be bent to serve our plans; they can be made into draft animals. To varying degrees the ideas and beliefs of others can be manipulated, changed, and remade. That is why the totalitarian regimes of the twentieth century were so insistent on having monopoly control over education, information, and entertainment. It is possible to influence (and sometimes radically) what people think, value, and want to live for. Since thinking, valuing, and living for one's self are not always easy to do, people often are receptive and susceptible to such "mind control."

Why is it a danger? Because no matter how confident and wise we may think we are, the fact remains that none of us knows enough to plan the lives of others. Our respective horizons of knowledge are too limited to even successfully plan our own lives. Long ago, Austrian economist and Nobel laureate Friedrich A. Hayek noted that matching the division of labor in society there is also an accompanying division of knowledge.[1] Each of us knows only a small fraction of all we need to know to achieve the ends and goals we try to attain. We rely upon the knowledge and abilities of far more people than we are aware of in the everyday affairs of life. From growing food, to manufacturing light bulbs, to inventing and constructing sophisticated tools and instruments in a research laboratory, the vast majority of us know absolutely nothing about how these things are done or how they or their results are made available to us on an everyday basis. Our individual degrees of ignorance are immense.

Hayek also emphasized that all this knowledge upon which we are dependent is not of one type. He distinguished at least three types of knowledge. The first is scientific or textbook knowledge—the type of knowledge that, in principle, with sufficient discipline and attention any individual could master. This is often the type of knowledge we acquire through formal schooling. But because of the time involved in learning and the amount of information that it is necessary to fully digest, each of us tends to become a "specialist" in only one or a small handful of such fields of knowledge.

Second is what Hayek called the particular and localized knowledge of time and place. This is the type of knowledge we acquire slowly through the experiences of working and living in a specific geographical location. The customs and methods of doing things in a particular business enterprise or social setting can only be known and learned "on the spot." Furthermore, this also involves the knowledge of changing circumstances specific to that location or place of business. What is relevant or useful today may not be tomorrow, and can only be known, appreciated, and effectively utilized by those "on the spot." Indeed, understanding why or how something may be relevant and useful at a particular moment or in a particular situation may be fully knowable only by those who are there and can see its relevance in the context of the pursuit of various purposes and plans.

The third type of knowledge is what Hayek, following the chemist and philosopher of science Michael Polanyi, called tacit or inarticulate knowledge.[2] This is knowledge about what to do, how and when, but it is a knowledge that individuals find difficult, sometimes impossible, to put down on paper, to convey into words, and share with others. Examples are the auto mechanic who can simply listen to an engine and "just know" what the problem is, or the master pottery-maker who "just knows" the right speed at which to turn the pottery wheel and the right amount of water to put on the clay to make it take form rather than fly off in all directions. Simple and mundane? No doubt. But much of what makes the world go round in everyday life depends upon those who bring to bear this "indescribable" knowledge, which we often take for granted.

Finally, following in the footsteps of Adam Smith and Carl Menger, the founder of the Austrian School of Economics, Hayek emphasized how many institutions of society are "the results of human action, but not of human design."[3] Whether it is a language, or customs, manners, and the unwritten and informal rules of social interaction, or the ideas concerning justice, fairness, and right and wrong, they have all emerged as the cumulative result of generations of people interacting. They have generated the sets of ideas and routinized way of doing things that we call the institutions of a society. Furthermore, they have evolved and taken the forms that they have with no one in earlier generations and ages knowing or planning how his or her actions in those past times might be a contributory element to the social order of our own time. As Hayek's mentor and fellow Austrian economist Ludwig von Mises once expressed it, "The historical process is not designed by individuals. It is the composite outcome of the intentional actions of all individuals. No one can plan history. All he can plan and try to put into effect is his own actions that, jointly with the actions of other men, constitute the historical process. The Pilgrim Fathers did not plan to found the United States."[4]

The limits and the different types of human knowledge and the nature and evolution of human institutions need to make all of us think twice before we proceed to impose our individual plans on others. Each individual's knowledge is confined to a small fraction of all the knowledge in the world, which resides as little bits in the separate minds of all members of humanity. To plan for others by making them conform to our plan for them is to restrict how they may use their own knowledge for themselves and for those with whom they would freely interact. It hinders what new knowledge and use of it they might uncover in their various everyday activities if they were at liberty to plan their own lives. We can never anticipate or appreciate in what ways that knowledge might have been applied to purposes that would have directly or indirectly benefited ourselves, if only we had not restricted other people's actions to a plan we imposed and that was limited to the knowledge that we possessed or which we might personally acquire in our own narrow corner of the world.[5]

Humility and self-interest, therefore, should make each of us resist the temptation to centrally plan for others in society. We should be respectful of each other as individual planners pursuing our respective ends, with the use of various chosen means. We should coordinate our individual plans through the interactions of the marketplace, through which we each have incentives and motives to apply our knowledge and abilities for the benefit of others so we may, in turn, obtain from others those things their knowledge can provide for us.

Alas, we humans seem to be constantly driven to plan other people's lives. Sometimes this is because people will not do things for us that we want done, or at least not at the terms we would prefer it to be provided. So we push for regulations and controls through government that will force others to do the things we want and at terms more to our liking. Or we use such regulations and controls to prevent others from competing against us in our corner of the market. Others are to be stopped from designing and implementing plans that would prevent our own plans from being carried out the way we want, even though their plans might be more attractive to potential trading partners than our own.

Sometimes we are driven to plan other people's lives because we know how they should live. We are shocked, disturbed, or frightened by the values or beliefs that others have and the way they live. Confident that we know the right values and beliefs and the proper or better way to live, we use the government to reeducate and reform others in society. We know how the institutions of the society should be redesigned or politically managed to herd our fellow men down the corridors of personal and social life that we just know will make them better and happier human beings.

Never is the lack of humility so great and the arrogance so inflated as when some are confident that they know how to plan the lives and socially engineer the institutions of another country. If it is impossible to have all the knowledge necessary, know all the institutional circumstances of one's own country and its people, as Hayek's arguments would strongly suggest, how even more impossible is it to claim to know enough to plan and engineer the redesigning and the remaking of another people and society halfway around the world?

How can a handful of people in Washington, D.C., for instance, understand the circumstances of tens of millions of people in a variety of foreign countries—their values, beliefs, and ideas about life and social relationships—with sufficient detail to attempt to remake their societies? How can they presume to have sufficient historical background and understanding of the special circumstances of those societies to know what political and social institutions need to be reformed? How can they know what shape and structure of reform would be compatible with the reality of the ideas, traditions, and political divisions of those countries?

The advantage acquired from a study of economics is that economists traditionally have been concerned precisely with drawing attention to the complex problems relating to social order and coordination. They have focused on the intricate network of human relationships through which the members of mankind interact with and benefit from one another's talents and abilities for purposes of mutual gains from trade. They have emphasized how the spontaneous orders of human society facilitate more flexibility and adaptability to unexpected change and innovation than any system of government regulation and control. They have drawn attention to the ability of coordinating the actions of billions of people in their production and consumption activities through the market system of competition and prices, and with far better result than any attempt at centralized planning and government command.

But while these have been some of the central questions and messages of economic analysis and public policy discourse by economists for well over two hundred years now, economists have not shared the same views or theoretical approaches to understanding the economic and political processes. These distinctions have sometimes suggested contradictions in the ideas and policy prescriptions among economists, but they have also often served as complementary contributions that have enriched our general understanding of the social, economic, and political world in which we live.

The 2003 Ludwig von Mises Lecture Series, held at Hillsdale College, was devoted to a presentation and comparison of some of these differing approaches to economic theory and public policy. The authors approached their subject with the idea of highlighting the contributions of a variety of economic schools of thought, and how they relate to other views on a number of subjects. Through these comparisons we will, it is hoped, come to a better and richer knowledge of the market order and its alternatives.

Ludwig von Mises, in whose name these lectures are delivered each year, clearly believed that economic understanding was a progressive process through which the contributions of each generation serve as the base for the next generation's additions of knowledge and insight. He said so rather clearly in explaining the relationship between the classical economists of the nineteenth century and the various proponents of "subjectivist" or marginal utility theory that is the foundation of modern microeconomics in its various formulations:

> The popular assertion that there are various schools of economics whose theories have nothing in common and that every economist begins by destroying the work of his predecessors in order to construct his own theory on its ruins is no more true than the other legends that the proponents of historicism, socialism and interventionism have spread about economics. In fact, a straight line leads from the system of the classical economists to the subjectivist [marginal utility] economists of the present. The latter is erected not on the ruins, but on the foundations, of the classical system. Modern economics has taken from its predecessors the best that it was able to offer. Without the work that the classical economists accomplished, it would not have been possible to advance to the discoveries of the modern school. . . . Everything that appears to those who have come afterward as a blind alley or at least as a wrong turning on the way to a solution was necessary in order to exhaust all possibilities and to explore and think through to its logical conclusion every consideration to which the problems might lead.[6]

It is with the hope of advancing such a growth in economic understanding that this year's Ludwig von Mises lectures are offered in printed form to the general public.

RICHARD M. EBELING
President
Foundation for
Economic Education
Irvington, New York

Notes

[1]Friedrich A. Hayek, "The Use of Knowledge in Society" [1945], reprinted in Richard M. Ebeling, ed., *Austrian Economics: A Reader* (Hillsdale, MI: Hillsdale College Press, 1990), pp. 226–46.

[2]Michael Polanyi, *Personal Knowledge* (Chicago: University of Chicago Press, 1958); *The Tacit Dimension* (New York: Doubleday, 1966).

[3]Friedrich A. Hayek, "The Results of Human Action but not of Human Design" [1967], in *Studies in Philosophy, Politics and Economics* (Chicago: University of Chicago Press, 1967), pp. 96–105; *Law, Legislation and Liberty*, Vol. 1: "Rules and Order" (Chicago: University of Chicago Press, 1973); and Carl Menger, *Investigations into the Methods of the Social Sciences with Special Reference to Economics* [1884] (New York: New York University Press, 1985), pp. 139–60, also reprinted in Richard M. Ebeling, ed., *Austrian Economics: A Reader*, pp. 183–211.

[4]Ludwig von Mises, *Theory and History: An Interpretation of Social and Economic Evolution* [1957] (Auburn, AL: Ludwig von Mises Institute, 1985), pp. 195–96.

[5]Friedrich A. Hayek, *The Constitution of Liberty* (Chicago: University of Chicago Press, 1962), pp. 22–38.

[6]Ludwig von Mises, "On the Development of the Subjective Theory of Value" [1931], in *Epistemological Problems of Economics* [1933] (New York: New York University Press, 1981), pp. 165–66.

JOSEPH A. STANISLAW

Controversies Among Free Marketers

I live in the world of enterprise where people make decisions. I work with governments who try to make decisions. I used to be an academic, but I am a practitioner now.

A few years ago, I used to say that the very beginning of the twenty-first century was not terribly different from the end of the nineteenth century and the beginning of the twentieth century. Three years ago, that sounded pretty good to me. I no longer like the comment.

What did the world look like at the end of the nineteenth century, the beginning of the twentieth century? There was unfettered global trade; technology was shrinking the world; the huge financial resources of the developed world were going to the developing countries—Argentina, India, China and, at that time, the United States. That world, however, was shattered by the guns of August 1914. It took until 1989, 1991, and the collapse of Communism to get the world back into a global marketplace. That is a long time to wait for real progress and prosperity. We now have open markets, we have, relatively speaking, free markets around the world.

However, the events of September 11, in some respects, happened because certain portions of the world are not open to ideas, are not open to free trade, are not open to the global world, the broader world. Let us hope that September 11 makes us all more willing to accept ideas, to accept trade, and to accept the movement of products in markets around the world. It marks the second modern era of the global economy from globalization to globality.

1

To tell this story of ideas, Daniel Yergin and I wrote *The Commanding Heights: The Battle for the World Economy*,[1] which is a story of the market, a story of the state. It is a story about whether governments or marketplace will be the driving force for making, reshaping, and redefining the world in which we live. (It is also the title of a PBS documentary, a six-hour series, which was shown last spring and which will be shown again this spring.)

I was inspired to write *Commanding Heights* for several reasons. One is what I learned while living in Europe from 1972 to 1997. My wife and I went there on our own because we wanted to be there—no company sent us. My education helped take us there as well. We lived in Great Britain from 1970 to 1980, which were eye-opening days. I was called a "don" then, a "fellow" at the University of Cambridge. To supplement my don's salary I was offered the opportunity to give one-hour seminars to students. I was paid £2.50 an hour at first; my fifth year, I was up to about £4 an hour. But what opened my eyes was the amount of money I took home to spend. Say I was making the equivalent of $6 an hour: I took home about a $1.50. Talk about destroying incentive or motivation! At one point I said, "Why do you even bother paying me, I'll just do it because I like doing it. There is no financial incentive here for me." At that time in Britain, at a very low-income level, the tax rate shot to over 50 percent, and then, at moderately higher income levels, it went even higher, toward 90 percent.

During my time in Great Britain there were many, many strikes. Two years running the entire country was shut down for three months. The system had gotten out of hand. It was state-owned, state-controlled. For example, if you wanted to buy a new stove (or cooker, as it is referred to there), you didn't have to make too many decisions because the government had already decided what color a stove should be and how many burners it should have. The car industry was nationalized. The government decided what color cars would be. (Not many cars were sold, by the way, because no one liked the colors. Eventually, the Japanese took over the market: They sold cars that people actually wanted to buy.)

Another reason I wanted to write the book came from my background. I grew up in northeastern Ohio, the Warren, Youngstown area, which had been the steelbelt of the United States. My father had been a steel worker, but the steel industry disappeared in the 1970s. People were fighting the market, fighting globalization, fighting the trend, trying to keep industries alive that couldn't compete in other parts of the world. What they should have been doing is figuring out how to retrain themselves, how to prepare themselves for other lines of work. Now, that may sound harsh; people like my father never went to school. He couldn't be retrained at the age of 55 or 60. But other, forward-looking things could have been done instead of fighting the inevitable disappearance of that industry as it was then structured in that area.

Finally, my own business convinced me we needed to write the book. My company has fourteen offices around the world, and we work with clients in over forty countries. The company, which we started in 1982, 1983, deals with energy—oil, gas, electricity, windmills, solar, hydropower. In the late 1980s, I began to realize that the prices of the energy commodities, oil or gas or electricity, were not the key and fundamental driving forces for the industry. What matters to industry was how the world was transforming itself. State-owned industries were about to unravel and unbundle and open markets to companies to invest in for the first time.

In Britain, in Europe, the electric power business and the natural gas business were state-controlled. They were being dismantled, however, and the private sector was allowed to move in. In addition, countries that had been closed to foreign investment and to any form of private investment, be it local or foreign investment, were now opening their doors to private capital. They were opening their markets for players and for competition. That was driving our industry, and our market outlook, and we had to know about that transformation. That, in large part, is why we wrote the book.

This new global economy exists because it needed to exist. The conventional wisdom of the 1950s, 1960s, and early 1970s was being criticized, discredited, and rethought. What was then considered the fringe by the majority of the people in the economic sphere, and beyond the fringe, began to move to center stage.

This was a move from an era of government control, of government seizing the commanding heights of the economy, to an era whose ideas hark back to the traditional liberalism of a century before—free

markets, competition, private companies—to capture the commanding heights of economic thinking. With that, the world was reordered.
Marxism was put aside. Entrepreneurism came full force, right into
the front. Socialists began to promote markets and capitalism.

A decade after Margaret Thatcher, as prime minister from the
Tory Party, promoted her principles they have become mainstream.
In the United States, a Democratic president, Bill Clinton, proclaimed
in his State of the Union Address, "The era of big government is over."

John Maynard Keynes was a macroeconomist who believed in
deficit spending, big government, and the idea that government creates demand and takes care of economic inadequacies. He said in
The General Theory of Employment, Interest and Money that ideas "are more
powerful than is commonly understood. Indeed, the world is ruled
by little else . . . sooner or later it is ideas, not vested interests, which
are the dynamics for good or evil."[2]

The story of ideas then moves from Keynesianism, which dominated thinking for decades, back to a school of thought that predates
Keynesianism: The Austrian School of economics is based in part on
the thinking of its most prominent member Ludwig von Mises, and
his critique in his book *Socialism.* Unfortunately, that book didn't take
hold strongly in 1922, when it was written. It is a brilliant analysis of
the failure of socialism, which went unnoticed for a while. Mises said
that socialism has to fail because it has no basis for rational decisions
to allocate resources. We have seen over the decades that this is true.[3]

A student of Mises, Friedrich Hayek, was instrumental in keeping Mises' ideas alive. Though often forgotten, it is interesting that it
was Keynes who helped Hayek do that. Keynes helped bring Hayek to
Britain, to Cambridge, during World War II. Although they were bit-
ter ideological enemies—Hayek was the first and most severe critic
of Keynes—they respected each other.

Hayek wrote *The Road to Serfdom, The Constitution of Liberty.* Laissez-faire, the free market, competition—Hayek says that's not enough,
you need a government, a referee with rules and laws by which people have to play.[4]

Hayek's ideas, however, have been dormant in the world of application, of policy. It was only recently, in the past two decades, that people have become ready and willing to adopt his ideas. In an interview

we did for *The Commanding Heights,* Milton Friedman explained the impact of free market ideas in the following way: "The role of people is to keep our ideas alive, until a crisis occurs. It wasn't my talking that caused people to embrace these ideas, just as a rooster doesn't make the sun rise. Collectivism was an impossible way to run an economy." What brought this change about is the reality of what Marx called the "inevitable forces of history." Lee Kuan Yew, who drove and defined the Singapore economic miracle, said simply, "Communism collapsed, the mixed economy failed, what else is there?"[5]

Part of the explanation of the move from government to state to marketplace is what we called the erosion of borders, the erosion of boundaries—the integration of economies, the drive to large regional markets such as the European Union. This was accompanied by technological development.

Technology is powerful. Telecommunications, for example, has advanced greatly in a short time. When we first went to Scotland in 1972, my wife and I could only afford to call home once a year at Christmas time. In today's dollars, it cost about $10 a minute to call the United States. Now it costs 30 cents a minute—or less. That is a revolution in telecommunications. Consider transportation. In 1972, it took ten hours to travel from Edinburgh to London by train. There was only one flight a day between the two cities. By the early 1980s, there were shuttles every thirty minutes. Technology makes a difference: Improved travel and communications allow capital to flow more quickly.

In a world that moves so fast, it becomes very hard for governments to keep pace. Does this mean we have a triumph of markets in the world? I think it means we are moving to test market principles, and to test the commitment to market principles. In Asia, we face challenges with testing these principles. We saw the 1998 crisis, the effects of which are still evident. Countries are afraid to open up and privatize, they are afraid of not being able to compete.

Europe is concerned about national identity as the market opens and competition takes place. In the United States I think we have to be concerned about the deficit, because it is getting bigger. Further, the move toward the marketplace that we have been witnessing over the past twenty years brings anxiety to people around the globe. There is fear that governments will not be there to protect them from the

uncertainties of the world. Many of us face the relentless demands of
the market, quarterly reporting, quarterly performance, fragility of
jobs—and that creates anxiety and different tensions.

How did we get to the "frontier" between the state government
and the marketplace? In the United States this change was driven by
the depression and World War II.

Someone from my industry, the energy industry, symbolizes the
failure of capitalism. Samuel Insull was an absolute genius, or at least
he was considered a genius in the 1920s. He built an electric power
empire that remains unmatched. He was the chairman of 65 corporations; he held 85 directorships; he was the president of 11 companies. He had massive economic power. He was considered to be
greedy and arrogant. When it all collapsed during the depression,
Franklin Roosevelt went after him. Insull became the villain of the
age, the symbol of all that had gone wrong with the market.

But the real villain was unemployment, instability, unfettered
capitalist greed. How did Roosevelt challenge this, how did he try
address it? He looked to Keynes, to Keynesianism; he looked to the
power of the state, deficit financing, and the government to create
aggregate demand. He did this through expanding regulation. The
United States became a regulated capitalist system.

In Europe, there is a mixed economy model, a welfare state,
government ownership, nationalization. In 1945 when Clement Attlee
became prime minister, he was determined to conquer unemployment, determined to end the class war in Britain; he wanted to wrest
control of the commanding heights of the economy from the large
industrialists.[6] To do that he nationalized.

In India, the Congress Party under Jawaharlal Nehru adopted a
notion of commanding heights for economic nationalism, so Indians
could gain control of their economy. Related to that was the drive to
wrestle economic control from the colonial powers, that is, from Britain.

A strong government takes responsibility for full employment.
World War II helped justify this approach. Survival played a critical
role. The ideas of the twenties were largely forgotten, though not by
the people of the Chicago School, but they weren't mainstream.

In the 1950s and 1960s, the Communist U.S.S.R. was thought to
be winning the economic and ideological battle. The Soviets were

experiencing higher growth than we were. At least we thought they were. That system seemed to be working better than ours at the time.

Let me give you an example of this thinking. Valérie Giscard d'Estaing, who was president of France from 1974 to 1981, was a junior minister under General Charles de Gaulle during the late fifties, early sixties. He was the youngest junior minister in French history. "When I went to school," he said, "there was no reference, no discussion whatsoever of the market or about the market." He added, "You have to understand that I was minister of the treasury under Charles de Gaulle. Remember who de Gaulle was: He was a general—and generals give orders. When he gave an order he expected you to deliver upon that order. . . . I realized things were going wrong with the French planned system when General de Gaulle told me that there would be no inflation in France. He told me 'no inflation.'" Giscard was in charge of keeping prices down, so he instituted price controls. To maintain those prices, he hired 3,000 people to go to every bakery in France every single week to make sure the price of bread didn't go up. "Something was not right," Giscard said. "This didn't seem the way to run the economy."[7] But, he was able to deliver to de Gaulle no inflation—but at a huge cost to resources, efficiency, and effectiveness. By the early 1970s it appeared that the government and the thinking around these Keynesian ideas had won the battle for the commanding heights. The policies that were used for two decades and the effects of those policies began to build up in the mid-1970s: inflation, large government deficits, large government debt, bankrupt state-owned companies, decades of wasted resources, inefficient use of capital.

C. H. Tung, the governor of Hong Kong, told me that Deng Xiaoping, the leader of China in the late seventies, decided to try to move his country toward a free market system. The reason he did this was very simple, as he indicated to Mr. Tung: "I only had two choices as the head of China. I can distribute poverty, or I can distribute wealth."[8] In two decades, Deng took three hundred million people out of poverty. Never before in the history of man has this been done.

Confidence that government had superior knowledge and ability was at its height in the early seventies. The most significant acknowledgment of government superiority occurred when *Time* magazine put John Maynard Keynes on the cover as "Man of the Year." (This was nineteen years after he had died.) That article basically said that economists can expertly manage the economy and can finetune it with Keynesian economics. If they can control aggregate demand and make sure that everything is okay, there would be full employment, no inflation. This was written just as the mixed economy, the basis of the 1950s, 1960s, and 1970s, began to fall apart. The welfare state got out of hand. It had become too big—and it kept growing. I witnessed this in Britain. Every day more was demanded and more was given: There was absolutely no way to pay for it, except through inflation and a declining standard of living.

A few short years after Keynes was named *Time*'s man of the year, the intellectual balance began to shift. In 1974 the Nobel Prize for Economics was awarded to two gentlemen: the Swedish economist Gunnar Myrdahl, a Keynesian, and Friedrich Hayek, Keynes's first and most important critic.

In the 1970s, the Austrian School slowly began moving into mainstream economic thought. In 1976, Milton Friedman won the Nobel Prize for economics. It was obvious that thinking was changing. The great reversal of what had been mainstream was galvanized by the election of Margaret Thatcher in 1979 and Ronald Reagan in 1980. Both preached the values of the market and pushed against big government.

Margaret Thatcher's acknowledged mentor had been Sir Keith Joseph.[9] Although some considered him a "quack," he resurrected the ideas of the Austrian School, of Hayek, of Mises through the Centre for Policy Studies. In 1974 he said that the conservatives had it all wrong, that they were fighting the wrong war. They worried about wealth distribution. They worried about how the government could solve all their problems. They had it wrong: There would be no wealth to distribute if they kept on that path. Basically he denounced the downward spiral, he personally drove the ideas of the marketplace, of competition, of reducing the welfare state, which then was powering the country. Joseph traveled on his own, he wrote his own speeches, he wrote his own books. He was booed; he was heckled; he was not mainstream. But he persisted; he was determined to make a change in Britain. Margaret Thatcher followed his lead and drove his cause. He was the intellectual mentor, not the driver. His work, and the work of others like him, reshaped the economy under Margaret Thatcher. They privatized industry, dismantled nationalized systems. They pulled back on the welfare state; they put competition back into play; they provided something called incentive. It is interesting that after Dr. Thatcher left, Prime Minister Tony Blair helped consolidate her revolution. He is driving it slightly differently, but he is still trying to drive it.

The complaints of the 1930s, 1940s, and 1950s about market failure became complaints of government failure. The government could not do all that it said it could. It could not solve the problems; the old Keynesian world could not work.

State-owned industry, which was meant to be the engine of modernization, became a political tool—corrupt, inefficient, and wasteful. Britain's debt crisis almost forced the country to bankruptcy. The Soviet Union collapsed under its own weight.

When I met the Indian economist G. V. Ramakrishna, he was in his mid-sixties and had been a career civil servant for forty years. He had headed the Indian State Planning Commission, which meant he was responsible for the planning of the entire Indian economy. He told me that after the Berlin Wall fell in 1989 and the U.S.S.R. came apart in 1991, it was like waking up from a 35-year-long nightmare. He said, "I looked in the mirror and realized that everything I had believed about the economic system, everything I tried to implement in India was wrong. . . . And I only have a few years left to try and change all that."[10] It became his mission to change India. He became chairman of the Disinvestment Commission. He tried to privatize many of the country's industries. That a man totally reverses his thinking after sixty-five years is significant.

As the red star was falling, a new star was rising in Asia. Many of us question whether the Asian economy was really a miracle of market principles. As Gary Becker, the Nobel laureate, put it, "By the world's standard at the time, Asia was pretty market-oriented.[11] And markets get better results than central planning.

Lawrence Summers, now president of Harvard, was secretary of the treasury under President Bill Clinton. He also happens to be the nephew of two Nobel Prize economists, Paul Samuelson and Kenneth Arrow. Without question, he is well-steeped in economic tradition. In his view, the invisible hand is more important than the hidden hand—things can happen in a well-organized way without controls, without planning. That is the Hayek legacy. As for Milton Friedman,

Larry Summers said, "He was a Devil figure in my youth. . . . Only with time have I come to have large amounts of grudging respect. And with time increasingly ungrudging respect."[12]

The 1997 report of the President's Council of Economic Advisers basically praised the advantages of the market and criticized and damned the "New Deal" because it crystallized a belief that the government could do everything and put the marketplace to the side. That was a pretty powerful statement for 1997. Structural changes contributed to this. There was lowering of trade barriers by the World Trade Organization to promote an open world economy. Technology facilitated the integration of capital markets, and these technological changes are irreversible. In Brazil in December 2002, following the election of President Luiz Inacio Lula da Silva, it was clear that Brazil would keep the market in place, but in a Brazilian way. A costly, several hundred million dollar communications satellite has been situated above Brazil to integrate it more effectively into the global economy.

Could there be a loss of confidence in markets? Can it go the other way? There is a lot of resentment against those who took advantage of the system, who became greedy—Enron, Arthur Andersen, WorldCom, Tyco, the list goes on and on. However our attachment to the marketplace is pragmatic—the market delivers the goods. And economic nationalism is still strong; it will have a role in how the market works. Asian countries, many of which have very little capital, are going to be reluctant to put themselves up completely for foreign direct investment.

Unemployment and downsizing is another major issue we have to address. We have to get economic growth going. As we move into this twenty-first century, romanticism, nostalgia, for yesterday's Golden Era is going to increase. When you have three bad years in a row, and maybe a fourth, nostalgia for the good old days gets stronger. But remember, people used to have very romantic views about horse and buggies, too. However, as the auto industry grew, more jobs were created, and the multiplier effect brought about more robust markets around the world; positive economic reality replaced nostalgic longings.

Today's world is a world of market discipline, but with differing degrees of government initiative. In *The Commanding Heights,* we describe five tests that will shape the future boundary between the state, government, and the marketplace. We are being tested right now. The first test is, will the market deliver the goods, meaning will it improve lifestyles, improve living standards? Second, is the system fair? Is it just? And does it need to be just and fair and equitable? How does it deal with overconcentrations of wealth and society's reactions to overconcentrations of wealth? As I said, after three bad economic years, resentment increases. Third, to what degree will the market allow national values, national history, national culture to be recognized? Fourth, how does the system of the marketplace deal with the public's perceptions about the environment? Finally, how does the system, the market, or the government deal with the demands and burdens of demographics? In the U.S., for example, we have an aging demographic. But the bulk of the world's population is young and unemployed. Peter Drucker said that the risks of a backlash of bitterness and contempt versus the rich, particularly in the U.S., when the business cycle turns down, is great. We know all too well that this is true.

One has to rethink the role of government as an active intervener because government doesn't have perfect wisdom. In Russia, in China, in India, they are struggling with how to construct a modern capitalist state. It is not easy.

In the U.S. and in Europe, we are trying to restructure social spending to create skills and jobs to compete in a global economy: If we don't, we can't compete. Our solution is more market, not more government. But, other countries need to determine what the solution will be for them. They are going to control the balance between the market principles and social stability. That is what President Lula is trying to do in Brazil. You have to address poverty in Brazil or that country will have no future. A realistic appraisal of risk, of uncertainty, and the benefits and value of markets vis-à-vis those risks and uncertainties must be done in each country on this road.

We can't go back. Technology goes forward; you can't put the genie back in the bottle. More information and open communication flows are necessary for the markets to work. Open markets create access to information and knowledge. That cannot be closed off.

Governments can slow all this, they can retard it, they can redirect it, but they can't stop it. The key to going forward successfully is to incorporate social values and social stability into the mix, to refocus regulation and to align the positive features of the market with social objectives, with the government as the referee on a well-defined, known, and transparent playing field.

Notes

[1]Daniel Yergin and Joseph Stanislaw, *The Commanding Heights: The Battle for the World Economy* (New York: Simon & Schuster, 1998, 2002).

[2]John Maynard Keynes, *The General Theory of Employment, Interest and Money* (London: Macmillan, 1936).

[3]Peter Klein, Ed., *The Fortunes of Liberalism: The Collected Works of F. A. Hayek,* vol. 4 (London: Routledge, 1992).

[4]F. A. Hayek, *The Constitution of Liberty* (London: Routledge, 1992)

[5]Lee Kuan Yew, discussion, International Institute for Strategic Studies meeting, Singapore, September 12, 1997.

[6]Kenneth Harris, *Atlee* (London: Weidenfeld & Nicolson, 1995).

[7]Interview with Valérie Giscard d'Estaing, *The Commanding Heights.*

[8]Interview with C. H. Tung, *The Commanding Heights.*

[9]*Richard Cockett, Thinking the Unthinkable: Think-Tanks and the Economic Counter-Revolution, 1931–1983* (London: Fontana Press, 1995).

[10]Interview with G. V. Ramakrishna, *The Commanding Heights.*

[11]Interview with Gary Becker, *The Commanding Heights.*

[12]Interview with Lawrence Summers, *The Commanding Heights.*

JAMES M. BUCHANAN

Public Choice: The Origins and Development of a Research Program

My subtitle identifies public choice as a research program rather than as a discipline or even a subdiscipline. (The Lakatosian definition seems to fit closely.) A research program incorporates acceptance of a hard core of presuppositions that impose limits on the domain of scientific inquiry while, at the same time, insulating such inquiry from essentially irrelevant criticism. The hard core in public choice can be summarized in three presuppositions: (1) methodological individualism, (2) rational choice, and (3) politics-as-exchange. The first two of these scientific building blocks are those that inform basic economics and will raise few criticisms from economists, although they become central in noneconomists' attacks on the whole enterprise. The third element in the hard core is less familiar, and I shall discuss this feature of public choice more fully later.

Temporally, this research program involves a half century during which it originated, developed, and matured. Although there were precursors, some of which will enter the narrative that follows, we can date the origins of public choice from mid-century. This fact, in itself, is of considerable interest. Viewed retrospectively, from the vantage point of 2003, the scientific-explanatory "gap" that public choice emerged to fill seems so large that the development of the program seems to have been inevitable.

A version of this paper was published as a monograph by the Center for Study of Public Choice, George Mason University, Fairfax, Virginia 22030.

13

As they emerged from World War II, governments, even in Western democracies, were allocating between one-third and one-half of their total product through collective-political institutions rather than through markets. Economists, however, were devoting their efforts almost exclusively to explanations—understandings of the market sector. No attention was being paid to political-collective decisionmaking. Practitioners in political science were no better. They had developed no explanatory basis, no theory as it were, from which operationally falsifiable hypotheses might be derived.

The entire politicized sector of social interaction was, therefore, "crying out" for explanatory models designed to help understand the empirical reality that was observed. My own piddling first entry into the subject matter (Buchanan, 1949) was little more than a call for those economists who examined taxes and spending to pay some attention to the models of politics that were assumed to be in existence. Except for the important, but neglected, paper by Howard Bowen, even those who made the recognized seminal contributions did not seem to appreciate the fact that they were entering uncharted territory.

Majority Cycles

Almost simultaneously, Duncan Black and Kenneth Arrow commenced their work on two quite separate problems, although their results converged with consequences that are by now familiar. Black was concerned with the working of majority-voting rules in small committee settings: How did voting results emerge from separate individual orderings, when collective alternatives (proposals, motions, etc.) were presented in a sequence of pairwise choices? Black found, to his surprise, that only two persons had worked out some of the elementary logic—the French nobleman Condorcet and Charles Dodgson, an Oxford logician more familiarly known under the name of Lewis Carroll. Duncan Black (1948, 1958), who was working in Wales, did not attract much early attention, either in his own country or elsewhere.

Kenneth Arrow sought to answer the question, Is it possible to aggregate separate individual orderings over social states so as to generate a "social" ordering that would satisfy reasonable conditions for rationality akin to those that characterized the individual orderings? Arrow commenced from within the tradition of what was then called "theoretical welfare economics." With the demolition of utilitarianism in 1932 at the hands of Lionel Robbins, economists rediscovered Pareto, but the Paretian classificatory scheme did not allow for a means of selecting among the many positions that met the criterion for Pareto efficiency or optimality. Using the formal tools of symbolic logic, Arrow reached the seemingly dramatic conclusion that no such social ordering may be derived unless some restrictions are placed on the individual preference orderings.

The now-famous "impossibility theorem," as published in Arrow's book *Social Choice and Individual Values* (1951), exerted a major impact on the thinking of economists and political scientists and stimulated an extended discussion. Arrow, and Black less emphatically, was taken to have shown that democracy, interpreted as equivalent to majority voting, could not work. Both of these scientists had discovered, or rediscovered, the phenomenon of majority cycles, and they rigorously demonstrated that, under some sets of preference orderings, majority voting in a sequence of pairwise comparisons would generate continuous cycles, with no equilibrium or stopping point.

The central point may be easily illustrated in the three-voter, three-alternative setting, as shown in Figure 1. Note that each of the three voters—labeled 1, 2, and 3—has a consistent ordering over the three options of choice—A, B, and C. Note also, however, that, when put to a pairwise sequence of majority votes, A will defeat B; B will, in turn, defeat C, but C will defeat A. There is no alternative that will command a majority over all of the other options.

Figure 1

1	2	3
A	B	C
B	C	A
C	A	B

Median Voter Models

Duncan Black, in particular, wanted to resuscitate the majority voting rule as the legitimate means of reaching group decisions. He discovered that if the alternatives for collective choice can be arrayed along a single dimension in such fashion that each voter's preferences exhibit single-peakedness, then the worrisome majority cycles would not occur. Instead, in this setting, the alternatives preferred by the voter whose preferences are median for the group would be majority-preferred to any other alternatives. This result, referred to as the *median voter theorem*, was quickly incorporated into both analytical and empirical research.

The single-peakedness required remains highly plausible in many settings. Suppose that the choice options, A, B, and C are alternative levels of spending on a collective outlay, say, on education. It is surely plausible that someone should prefer high spending (A), to medium spending (B), to low spending (C), hence the ordering for the first voter in Figure 1. It is also plausible that a voter, say 2, might prefer medium spending (B) to low spending (C), and this in turn to high spending (A), the ordering shown for the second voter. But look at the ordering for the third voter in Figure 1. This voter prefers low spending (C), but her second choice is high spending (A), which she prefers over medium spending (B), which seems a rather bizarre ordering in some settings. Yet it is precisely such anomalies in orderings that are necessary to generate the majority voting cycles. The median voter theorem seemed initially to be explanatory over wide ranges of collective action.

It was evident early on, however, and also had been recognized by Black himself, that once collective choices involve more than a single dimension, majority cycles must occur even if all voters exhibit single-peakedness in preferences over each of the dimensions considered separately. Majority voting seemed to be basically unstable in the sense that it could not produce a unique collective choice; a political equilibrium could not be reached.

Is Collective Rationality Desirable?

It was at this point that I entered the discussion with a generalized critique of the whole corpus of analysis generated by the Arrow-Black approach (Buchanan, 1954a, 1954b). If, indeed, preferences differ over collective alternatives, and if these preferences are such as to generate cycles in voting outcomes, would not this result be precisely that which is best? Any attainment of a unique solution by majority voting would amount to the permanent imposition of the majority's will on the outvoted minority. Would not a guaranteed rotation, as produced through the cycle, be the preferred sequence here? In such a cyclical sequence, the members of the minority in the first round are enabled to come back in subsequent rounds and ascend to majority membership. My concern, then and later, was always with means of preventing discrimination against members of minorities rather than insuring that, somehow, majority rule produced stable sets of political outcomes.

Examined from an economist's perspective, what guarantee could majority rule offer against collective actions that were inefficient in the standard Pareto sense? Clearly, the natural feature of majority voting is the separation of the interests of members of the majority from those of the minority. On any single voting sequence, some persons in the inclusive polity must lose and others must gain. How can collective choice be made more efficient? And more just?

Wicksell and the Rule of Unanimity

At this point, I introduce the great Swedish economist Knut Wicksell, who is the most important of all precursory figures in public choice, especially for my own work and for what we now call *constitutional economics*. In his dissertation published in 1896 (Wicksell, 1896), Wicksell was concerned about both the injustice and the inefficiency of untrammeled majority rule in parliamentary assemblies. He did not discover the possibility of the majority cycle, but he did recognize that majorities were quite likely to enact legislation aimed at benefiting the constituencies of their own members at the expense of those members left outside the majority coalitions. Majority rule seemed quite likely to impose net costs or damages on large segments of the taxpayer-beneficiary group. Why should members of such minorities, facing discrimination, lend their support to political structures? Unless all groups can, somehow, benefit from the ultimate exchange with the government, how can overall stability be maintained?

These considerations led Wicksell to question the efficacy of majority rule itself. To ensure both enhanced efficiency and increased justice in the fundamental dealings of the individual with governmental authority (the state), Wicksell proposed that the voting rule be modified in the direction of unanimity. If the agreement of all persons in the voting group should be required to implement collective action, then this result, in itself, would guarantee that all persons secure net gains and, further, that the projects so approved yield, overall, benefits in excess of costs.

Wicksell recognized that, if applied in a literal voting setting, a requirement of unanimity would produce stalemate, since it allows each and every person to play off against all others in the group. Such a recognition does not, however, change the value of the unanimity rule as a benchmark for comparative evaluation. In suggestions for practical constitutional reforms, Wicksell supported changes in voting rules from simple to qualified majorities, perhaps, for example, the requirement of five-sixths approval for collective proposals.

My own serendipitous discovery of Wicksell's neglected work in 1948, followed by my later translation of this work from German, introduced the important contribution to English-language scholars, and laid the groundwork for later developments in constitutional economics, which I shall discuss more fully below.

The Endogeneity of Alternatives

In their analyses, Black and Arrow had assumed, more or less implicitly, that the alternatives for collective choice, among which the voting rule generates an outcome, are exogenous to the process itself, that is, that the motions, candidates, or proposals exist prior to the selection process itself. For Wicksell, this exogeneity could not be present, but he did not, himself, recognize the relevance of this difference.

Gordon Tullock, with whom I began to work at the University of Virginia in 1958, wrote a seminal paper on majority rule in 1959 (Tullock, 1959), which made the endogeneity of the choice options a central feature, although, even here, he did not recognize the generality of the distinction. Tullock's example was that of farmers-voters, each of whom wants to have his local road repaired with costs borne by the whole community of taxpayers. Majority-voting rules, as these allow for separate coalitions of farmers, generate results that impose costs on all farmers, while producing inefficiently large outlays on all local roads. These results emerge because majority-voting rules, as the institutions for making collective choices, allow any and all potential coalitions to advance taxing-spending proposals endogenously—proposals that would never arise from outside, so to speak.

The Calculus of Consent

If majority-voting rules operate so as to produce inefficient and unjust outcomes, and if political stability is secured only by discrimination against minorities, how can democracy, as the organizing principle for political structure, possibly claim normative legitimacy? The Wicksellian criterion for achieving justice and efficiency in collective action, namely the shift from majority-voting rules toward unanimity, seems institutionally impractical. But, without some such reform, how could persons as voters-taxpayers-beneficiaries be ensured that the ultimate exchange with the state yield net benefits? That the whole game of politics be positive sum?

At this point, and in implicit response to these questions, Gordon Tullock and I commenced to work on what was to become our book *The Calculus of Consent,* published in 1962. The central contribution of our book was to impose a two-level structure of collective decisionmaking; we distinguished between what may be called "ordinary politics" (indicated by decisions made, often by majority voting, in legislative assemblies) and "constitutional politics" (indicated by decisions made on the set of framework rules within which the operation of ordinary politics is allowed to proceed). We were not, of course, inventing this two-level distinction as descriptive of political reality; both in legal theory and in practice, constitutional law had long been distinguished from statute law. What we did was to bring this quite familiar distinction into the corpus of the theoretical analysis of politics, the research program that was just on the verge of being developed in the 1950s and 1960s.

This distinction allowed us to answer the questions posed previously. Less-than-unanimity rules, and even majority rules, may be allowed to operate over the decisions made through ordinary politics provided that there is generalized consensus on the "constitution," on the inclusive set of framework rules that place boundaries on what ordinary politics can and cannot do. In this fashion, the analysis in *The Calculus of Consent* made it possible to incorporate the Wicksellian reform thrust toward qualified or super-majorities into politics at the level of constitutional rules, while allowing for ordinary majority-voting rules within constitutional limits.

In a sense, the whole analysis in our book could have been interpreted as a formalization of the structure that James Madison had in mind when he constructed the United States Constitution. Or, at the least, the analysis offered a substantive criticism of the then-dominant elevation of majority voting to sacrosanct status in political science.

The Public Choice Society and *Public Choice*

Our book was well-received by both economists and political scientists. Through the decades since its publication, the book has achieved status as a seminal work in the research program. The initial interest in the book, and its arguments, prompted Gordon Tullock and me, who were then at the University of Virginia, to initiate and organize a small research conference in Charlottesville in April 1963. We brought together economists, political scientists, sociologists, and scholars from other disciplines, all of whom were engaged in research outside the boundaries of their disciplines. The discussion was sufficiently stimulating to motivate the formation of a continuing organization, which we first called the Committee on Non-Market Decision-Making, and to initiate plans for a journal initially called *Papers on Non-Market Decision-Making*, which Gordon Tullock agreed to edit.

We were all unhappy with these awkward labels, but after several annual meetings there emerged the new name *public choice*, both for the organization and the journal. In this way the Public Choice Society and the journal *Public Choice* came into being. Both have proved to be quite successful as institutional embodiments of the research program, and sister organizations and journals have since been set up in Europe and Asia.

William Riker, who organized some of the early meetings, exerted a major influence on American political science through the establishment and operation of the graduate research program at the University of Rochester. Second- and even third-generation Riker students occupy major positions throughout the country and carry forward the research thrust in positive political analysis.

In the late 1960s, both Gordon Tullock and I shifted to Virginia Polytechnic and State University, and in Blacksburg we set up the Center for Study of Public Choice, which served as an institutional home, of sorts, for visiting research scholars throughout the world. This center, and its related programs, operated effectively until 1983, when it was shifted to George Mason University, where its operation continues.

I shall not discuss in detail the institutional history of the society, the journal, the center, and related organizations. Suffice it to say here that these varying structures reflect the development and maturing of the whole research program.

Subprograms and Rent-Seeking

I shall not discuss the separate research subprograms that have emerged within public choice as the umbrella subdiscipline. Note may be made only of some, but by no means all, of these subprograms: Riker's early work on coalition formation in legislatures (Riker, 1962) was the focus of early attention; the economic analysis of anarchy attracted much effort in the early 1970s (Tullock, 1972, 1974a, 1974b; Buchanan, 1975); agenda manipulation as a means of controlling political outcomes (Romer and Rosenthal, 1978); Mancur Olson's logic of collective action (Olson, 1965); James Coleman's exchange-based social action (Coleman, 1990); explanations for the growth of government; theories of bureaucracy; structure-induced equilibria in politics; expressive versus interest voting; the role of ideology. These and other subprograms emerged from within public choice, quite apart from the more familiar programs upon which analysis was brought to bear, such as unicameral versus bicameral legislatures, legislative committee structures, proportional versus plurality systems, direct democracy, size of legislatures, federalism, and many others.[1]

One subprogram that emerged from within public choice deserves specific, if necessarily brief, discussion here. I refer to rent-seeking, a subprogram initiated in a seminal paper by Gordon Tullock in 1967, and christened with this title by Anne Krueger in 1974. At base, the central idea emerges from the natural mind-set of the economist, whose explanation of interaction depends critically on the predictable responses of persons to measurable incentives. If an opportunity that promises to yield value arises, persons will invest time and resources in efforts to capture such value for themselves. The market itself is a profit-and-loss system; resources tend to move to their most highly valued uses because persons can be predicted to respond positively to promised profit opportunities and negatively to threatened losses.

The extension of this motivational postulate to the share of value allocated through politics or collective action seems elementary now, but until Gordon Tullock explicitly made the connection, no attention had been paid to the profound implications: If there is value to be gained through political action, persons will invest resources in efforts to capture this value. And if this value takes the form of any transfer from one group to others, the investment is wasteful in an aggregate value sense.

Gordon Tullock's early treatment of rent-seeking was concentrated on monopoly, tariffs, and theft, but the list could be almost indefinitely expanded. If the government is empowered to grant monopoly rights or tariff protection to one group, at the expense of the general public or to designated losers, then it follows that potential beneficiaries will compete for the prize, so to speak. Since by construction, only one group can be rewarded, the resources invested by other groups are wasted. These resources could have been used to produce valued goods and services.

Once this basic insight is incorporated into the mind-set of the observer, much of modern politics can only be interpreted as rent-seeking activity. The pork-barrel politics of the United States is only the most obvious example. Much of the growth of the transfer sector of government can best be explained by the behavior of political agents who compete in currying constituency support through promises of discriminatory transfers.

The subprogram remains active along several dimensions. How much value, in the aggregate, is dissipated through efforts to use political agency for essentially private profit? How can the activity of rent-seeking, as aimed to secure discriminatory private gains, be properly distinguished from the activity aimed to further genuinely shared "public" interests? I shall not go into detail here, but it should be clear that rent-seeking, as a subprogram in public choice more generally, opens up many avenues for both analytical and empirical inquiry.

Constitutional Political Economy

I noted earlier that the primary contribution of the book *The Calculus of Consent* was to impose a two-level framework on analyses of collective action or to distinguish categorically what we may call ordinary or day-do-day politics from constitutional politics. Indeed the subtitle of that book was *Logical Foundations of Constitutional Democracy*. In a sense, this separation marked a major two-part division in the inclusive research program in public choice, that is, between what we might call positive political analysis, or positive public choice, and what we now call *constitutional political economy*.

Clearly, political-collective action, as resultant from individual choices, takes place at two or more distinct stages or levels. There are, first, the choices made within the existing set of rules, inclusively described as the "constitution." There are, second, the choices from which these rules themselves emerge. Rules have as their primary function the imposition of limits or constraints on actions that might be taken. Economic theory, traditionally, has analyzed choices made within constraints that are presumed to be exogenously imposed. Why should persons seek to impose limits on their own actions?

Only recently have economists broken out of their natural mindset—that of not allowing for choices of constraints themselves. But recent research has involved the choice of constraints, even on the behavior of persons in noncollective settings. Important contributions have been made in developing the theory of addiction, with drugs, tobacco, food, and gambling as relevant examples. The issues become categorically different, however, as attention is shifted from the noncollective or individualistic setting to that involving collective rules.[2] In this setting, persons desire to impose constraints on the behavior of agents who act on behalf of the political group, not from any fear of irrational behavior on their own part, but instead from the fear of the prospect that their own preferences will be overruled, that their own interests will be damaged. Constitutional rules have as their central purpose the imposition of limits on the potential exercise of political authority.

The "constitutional way of thinking" (Buchanan, 2001) shifts attention to the framework rules of political order as the object that commands or secures consensus among members of the body politic. It is at this level that the individual conceptually computes or calculates his own terms of exchange with the state, or with political authority. Persons may agree that they are made better off by membership in the inclusive structure described by the constitution, while at the same time they may assess the impact of particular political actions to be contrary to their own interests. A somewhat loose way of putting this point is to say that in a constitutional democracy persons owe loyalty to the constitution rather than to the government, as such, no matter how "democratic" such decisions might be. I have long argued that on precisely this dimension American public attitudes are quite different from those in Europe.

As research analysis, constitutional political economy involves comparative assessment of alternative sets of constitutional rules, both those in existence and those that might be introduced prospectively. This analysis clearly has close affinity to the recent efforts to introduce the study of institutions, generally. There are, of course, both positive and normative elements in this major research program. Differing sets of rules are examined and predictions are advanced concerning their working properties. From such analysis proposals for reform may be advanced—proposals that take the form of constitutional changes, as opposed to proposals for particularized policy thrusts that might emerge from analysis of ordinary or within-constitutional politics.

Is Public Choice Ideologically Biased?

To this point, I have outlined the public choice research program as it has developed and as it now exists in its two parts, that of positive political science and constitutional political economy. How does the politics that we observe work, given the existing constitutional structure? And how might politics be different under differing sets of constitutional constraints? In its approach to answers to each of these questions, public choice theory, as such, remains strictly neutral in the scientific sense. What, then, is the source of the familiar criticism to the effect that public choice, in itself, is ideologically biased?

Again, it is necessary to appreciate the prevailing mind-set of social scientists and philosophers at mid-century. The socialist ideology was pervasive, and this ideology was supported by the allegedly neutral research program called *theoretical welfare economics,* which concentrated on the identification of the failures of observed markets to meet idealized standards. In sum, this branch of inquiry offered theories of market failure. But failure by comparison with what? The implicit presumption was always that politicized corrections for market failures would work perfectly. In other words, market failures were set against an idealized politics.

Public choice then came along and provided analyses of politics, of the behavior of persons in public choosing roles whether these be voters, politicians, or bureaucrats, that were on all fours with those applied to markets and to the behavior of persons as participants in markets. These analyses necessarily exposed the essentially false comparison that had described so much of both scientific and public attitudes. In a very real sense, public choice became a set of theories of governmental failures, as an offset to the theories of market failures that had previously emerged from theoretical welfare economics. Or, as I put it in the title of a lecture in Vienna in 1978, public choice may be summarized by the three-word description "politics without romance."

The research program should have been interpreted as a correction more of the scientific record than as the introduction of some illegitimate anti-governmental ideology. Regardless of any prescientific ideological stance, exposure to public choice analyses necessarily brings a more critical attitude toward politicized nostrums to alleged socioeconomic problems and issues. Public choice almost literally forces the critic to be pragmatic in any comparison of proposed institutional structures. There can be no presumption that politicized corrections for market failures will accomplish the desired objectives.

Is Public Choice Immoral?

A more provocative criticism of the whole public choice research program centers on the claim that it is immoral, at least in its behavioral impact. The source of this charge lies in the transfer of the two hardcore elements, methodological individualism and rational choice, directly from economic theory to the analysis of politics. At one level of abstraction, these two elements are themselves relatively empty of empirical content. To model the behavior of persons, whether in markets or in politics, as maximizing utilities, and as behaving rationally in so doing, does not require specification of the arguments in utility functions. Economists go further than this initial step, however, when they identify and place arguments into the categories of "goods" and "bads." Persons are then modeled as acting so as to maximize some index of "goods," while minimizing some index of "bads."

More specifically, economic models of behavior include net wealth, an externally measurable variable, as an important "good" that persons seek to maximize. The moral condemnation—criticism of public choice—is centered on the presumed transference of this element of economic theory over to political analysis. Those who find themselves in roles as public choosers, whether as voters, as legislators, as political agents of any sort, do not, it is suggested, behave in accordance with norms that are appropriate to behavior in markets. Persons are differently motivated when they are choosing "for the public" rather than for themselves in private choice capacities. And it is both descriptively inaccurate and morally questionable to assign self-interest motives to political actors. Or so the criticism runs.

At base, this criticism stems from a misunderstanding of what the explanatory exercise is all about—a misunderstanding that may have been fostered by the failure of economists to acknowledge the limits of their efforts. The economic model of behavior, even if restricted to market activity, should never be taken to provide the be-all and end-all of scientific explanation. Persons act from many motives, and the economic model concentrates attention only on one of the many possible forces behind actions. To employ the model for prediction does, of course, require the initial presumption that the identified "goods" that are maximized are relatively important in the mix. Hypotheses that imply that promised shifts in net wealth modify behavior in predictable ways have not been readily falsifiable empirically.

At issue here is the degree to which net wealth, and promised shifts in net wealth, may be used as explanatory incentives for the behavior of persons in public choice roles. Public choice, as an inclusive research program, incorporates the presumption that persons do not readily become economic eunuchs as they shift from market to political participation. The person who responds predictably to ordinary incentives in the marketplace does not fail to respond at all when his role is shifted to collective choice. The public choice theorist should, of course, acknowledge that the strength, and predictive power, of the strict economic model of behavior is somewhat mitigated as the shift is made from private market to collective choice. Persons in political roles may, indeed, act to a degree in terms of what they consider to be the general interest. Such acknowledgment does not, however, in any way imply that the basic explanatory model loses all of its predictive potential, or that ordinary incentives no longer matter.

What is left of the charge of immorality, once this much is acknowledged? Critics are somehow left with the claim that persons placed in political or public choice roles will themselves be led to act as the economic model dictates if such models are used in the inclusive explanatory exercise. In this light, it becomes immoral to model political choice behavior as being responsive to ordinary incentives, even if such an exercise is admittedly partially explanatory.[3] We should, therefore, proceed with analysis of politics under the illusion that persons do, indeed, become "saints" as they shift to collective choice roles. The positive value of hypocrisy may be recognized, but without elevating hypocrisy to an instrumental status in preserving social stability. Democracy, or self-government generally, is surely strong enough to allow for honesty in analysis of its own workings.

Balancing the Accounts

As noted, public choice as a research program has developed and matured over the course of a full half century. It is useful to assess the impact and effects of this program, both on thinking in the scientific community and in the formation of public attitudes. By simple comparison with the climate of opinion at half century, both the punditry and the public are much more critical of politics and politicians, much more cynical about the motivations of political action, much less naive in thinking that political nostrums offer easy solutions to social problems. This shift in attitudes extends well beyond the loss of belief of the efficacy in central planning, in socialism—a loss of belief grounded both in historical regime failures and collapse of intellectually idealized structures.

The question to be examined is not whether attitudes toward politics and politicians have shifted, often dramatically, over the half century. The question is instead, What contribution has the research program of public choice brought to this attitudinal change?

As I noted earlier, when we look retrospectively at the scientific and public climates of discussion at mid-century, the failure of social scientists to make efforts to understand and explain decisionmaking in the proportionately large collectivized sector of social interaction seems difficult to comprehend. The gap in scientific effort now seems so obvious that the development of public choice, and related programs, becomes a natural and indeed necessary step in our always incomplete knowledge about the world. Nonetheless, there were two obstacles to be overcome in the intellectual community—obstacles that were, strangely, both opposites and complements.

Broadly considered, the prevailing mind-set was socialist in the underlying presupposition that politics offered the solution to social problems. But there was a confusing amalgam of Marxism and ideal political theory involved: Governments, as observed, were modeled by Marxists as furthering class interests, but governments that might be installed "after the revolution," so to speak, would become both omniscient and benevolent.

In some of their implicit modeling of political behavior aimed at furthering special group or class interests, the Marxists seemed to be closet associates in public choice, even as they rejected method-ological individualism. But how was the basic Marxist critique of pol-itics, as observed, to be transformed into the idealized politics of the benevolent and omniscient superstate? This question was simply left glaringly unanswered. The calculation debates of the 1930s, consid-ered, by confused economists of the time, to have been won by social-ists over Mises and Hayek embodied the neglect, to an extent by both sides, of the relevance of incentives in motivating human action, in-cluding action in the politicized sector.

The structure of ideas that were adduced in support of the emerg-ing Leviathan welfare state was logically flawed and could have been maintained only through long-continued illusion. But, interestingly, the failure, in whole or in part, of the socialist structure of ideas did not come from within the scientific academy. Mises and Hayek were not successful in their early efforts, and classical liberalism seemed to be at its nadir at mid-century. Failure came, not from a collapse of an intellectually defunct structure of ideas, but from the cumulative record of nonperformance in the implementation of extended collec-tivist schemes—nonperformance measured against promised claims, something that could be observed directly. In other words, govern-ments everywhere, both in the socialist and welfare states, overreached themselves, and tried to do more than the institutional framework would support. This record of failure came to be recognized widely, commencing in the 1960s and accelerating in the 1970s.

Where was the influence of public choice in this history? Note specifically that I do not claim that public choice, as a coherent set of scientifically based theories of how politics works in practice, dislodged the prevailing socialist mind-set in the academies and that some sub-sequent recognition of the intellectual vulnerability exerted its feed-back on political reality. In common parlance, public choice was not "ahead of the curve" in this respect.

What I do claim is that public choice exerted its influence, which was major, in the provision of a coherent understanding and inter-pretation of that which could be everywhere observed. The public directly observed that collectivistic schemes were failing, that politici-zation did not offer the promised correctives for any and all social ills, that governmental intrusions often made things worse rather than better. How could these direct observations be fitted into a satisfactory understanding? Why did the nostrums promised fail to deliver?

Public choice came along and offered a foundation for such an understanding. Armed with nothing more than the rudimentary insights from public choice, persons could understand why, once established, bureaucracies tend to grow apparently without limit and without connection to initially promised functions. They could understand why pork-barrel politics dominate the attention of legislators; why there seems to be a direct relationship between the overall size of government and the investment in efforts to secure special concessions from government (rent-seeking); why the tax system is described by the increasing number of special credits, exemptions, and loopholes; why balanced budgets are so hard to secure; why strategically placed industries secure tariff protection.

A version of the old fable about the king's nakedness may be helpful here. Public choice is like the small boy who said that the king really has no clothes. Once he said this, everyone realized that the king's nakedness had been recognized, but that no one had called attention to the fact. Public choice has helped the populace take off their rose-colored glasses when they observe the behavior of politicians and the working of politics.

Let us be careful not to claim too much, however. Public choice did not emerge from some profoundly new insight, some new discovery, some social science miracle. Public choice, in its basic insights into the workings of politics, incorporates a presupposition about human nature that differs little, if at all, from that which informed the thinking of James Madison at the American founding. The essential scientific wisdom of the eighteenth century, of Adam Smith and classical political economy and of the American founders, was lost through two centuries of intellectual folly. Public choice does little more than incorporate a rediscovery of this wisdom and its implications into analyses and appraisal of modern politics.

Notes

[1]For a comprehensive treatment that includes discussion of the subprograms in public choice, see Mueller (1989).

[2]For general discussion, see Brennan ánd Buchanan (1985).
[3]See Kelman (1987) and Brennan and Buchanan (1988).

References

Arrow, Kenneth. *Social Choice and Individual Values* (New York: Wiley, 1951).
Black, Duncan. "On the Rationale of Group Decision Making," *Journal of Political Economy* 56 (1948): 23–34.
_____. *The Theory of Committees and Elections* (Cambridge: Cambridge University Press, 1958).
Bowen, Howard. "The Interpretation of Voting in the Allocation of Economic Resources," *Quarterly Journal of Economics* 58 (November 1943): 27–49.
Brennan, Geoffrey and James M. Buchanan. *The Reason of Rules: Constitutional Political Economy* (Cambridge: Cambridge University Press, 1985).
_____. "Is Public Choice Immoral? The Case for the 'Nobel' Lie," *Virginia Law Review* 74 (March 1988): 179–89.
Buchanan, James M. "The Pure Theory of Government Finance: A Suggested Approach," *Journal of Political Economy* 57 (December 1949): 496–505.
_____. "Social Choice, Democracy, and Free Markets," *Journal of Political Economy* 62 (April 1954a): 114–23.
_____. "Individual Choice in Voting and the Market," *Journal of Political Economy* 62 (August 1954b): 334–43.
_____. *The Limits of Liberty: Between Anarchy and Leviathan* (Chicago: University of Chicago Press, 1975).
_____. "Politics without Romance: A Sketch of Positive Public Choice Theory and Its Normative Implications," Inaugural Lecture, Institute for Advanced Studies, Vienna, Austria, *IHS Journal, Zeitschrift des Instituts für Höhere Studien* 3 (Wien, 1979): B1–B11.
_____. "The Constitutional Way of Thinking," (Fairfax, VA: Center for Study of Public Choice, George Mason University, 2001), working paper.
Buchanan, James M. and Gordon Tullock. *The Calculus of Consent: Logical Foundations of Constitutional Democracy* (Ann Arbor: University of Michigan Press, 1962).
Coleman, James. *Foundations of Social Theory* (Cambridge, MA: Harvard University Press, 1990).
Kelman, Steven. "'Public Choice' and Public Spirit," *Public Interest* 87 (1987): 93–94.
Krueger, Anne. "The Political Economy of the Rent-Seeking Society," *American Economic Review* 64 (June 1974): 291–303.
Mueller, Dennis. *Public Choice II* (Cambridge: Cambridge University Press, 1989).
Olson, Mancur. *The Logic of Collective Action* (Cambridge, MA: Harvard University Press, 1965).

Riker, William. *The Theory of Political Coalitions* (New Haven, CT: Yale University Press, 1962).

Romer, Thomas and Howard Rosenthal. "Political Resource Allocation, Controlled Agendas, and the Status Quo," *Public Choice* 33(1978): 27–43.

Tullock, Gordon. "Problems of Majority Voting," *Journal of Political Economy* 67 (December 1959): 571–79.

_____. "The Welfare Costs of Tariffs, Monopolies, and Theft," *Western Economic Journal* 5 (June 1967): 224–32.

_____, ed. *Explorations in the Theory of Anarchy* (Blacksburg, VA: Center for Study of Public Choice, 1972).

_____. *The Social Dilemma: The Economics of War and Revolution* (Blacksburg, VA: Center for Study of Public Choice, 1974a).

_____, ed. *Further Explorations in the Theory of Anarchy* (Blacksburg, VA : Center for Study of Public Choice, 1974b).

Wicksell, Knut. *Finanztheoretische Untersuchungen* (Jena: Gustav Fisher, 1896); in *Classics in the Theory of Public Finance,* R. A. Musgrave and A. T. Peacock, eds. (New York: St. Martin's Press, 1958): 72–118.

Richard M. Ebeling

Man, Meaning, and the Market Process: The Ethos of the Austrian School of Economics

The revival of the modern Austrian School of economics may be dated from the week of June 15 to 22, 1974, when the Institute for Humane Studies sponsored a conference on "Austrian Economics" for about forty participants in the small New England town of South Royalton, Vermont. For almost a quarter of a century the Austrian School had been in hiatus. The rise and then triumph of Keynesian economics in the late 1930s and 1940s as an explanation of and policy prescription for events like the Great Depression of the early 1930s eclipsed all competing theories and practical solutions to problems of high unemployment and the business cycle. This included the Austrian theory of the business cycle, which in the first half of the 1930s had been a leading alternative to the emerging Keynesian theory of macroeconomics.[1]

At the same time, there developed what came to be called the neoclassical approach in microeconomics. The study of the logic of individual decisionmaking, the allocation of scarce resources among competing uses, and the distribution of income among the factors of production—land, labor, and capital—became increasingly an exercise in mathematical optimization under conditions of various constraints. The focus of attention was on the specification and determination of the narrow and often highly artificial conditions under which the market economy as a whole would be in a state of full and complete general equilibrium. This, too, was in stark contrast to the approach of many Austrian economists, who were attempting to ex-

plain the processes of market competition, and adaptation and adjustment to a world of continual change, regardless of whether some
hypothetical state of equilibrium was even possible or ever to actually
occur.

Before the 1940s, the Austrian economists had been considered
one of the most original groups of thinkers and contributors to economic theory and policy for more than sixty years. They were among
the leading developers of the theory of marginal utility, opportunity
cost, value and price, capital and interest, market theory and the price
system, monetary and business cycle theory, and comparative economic systems—capitalism versus socialism versus the interventionist–welfare state.[2]

In October 1973, eight months before that conference in South
Royalton, the most important contributor to Austrian economics
in the twentieth century, Ludwig von Mises, had died at the age of
ninety-two.[3] The second most prominent member of the Austrian
School at that time, Friedrich A. Hayek, had been invited to attend
the conference, but had declined due to health problems that made
it impossible for him to travel to America from Europe. No one at the
conference anticipated that only four months later, in October 1974,
Hayek would be awarded the Nobel Prize in Economics.[4]

The speakers at the conference were three other leading figures
in Austrian economics: Ludwig M. Lachmann, who had studied with
Hayek at the London School of Economics in the 1930s; Israel M.
Kirzner, who had studied with and written his dissertation under
Mises at New York University in the late 1950s;[5] and Murray N. Rothbard, who had attended Mises' New York University seminar for many
years in the 1950s and had received his doctoral degree in economics
from Columbia University. Most of the forty attendees were in their
twenties or early thirties: They were either still in graduate school or
had just earned their own advanced degrees.[6]

To my best recollection, I was the only undergraduate invited to
the conference. After serving briefly in the United States Navy, I had
returned to school and was still two years away from my bachelor's
degree in economics. The Institute for Humane Studies had kindly
paid my way from California, where I was living, to the conference in
Vermont—via Greyhound Bus! For three and a half days, in both

directions, I had the opportunity to vividly see the logic and content of various bizarre forms of human action in practice among my fellow bus passengers.

One evening during the conference, Milton Friedman came from his summer home in Vermont to join us for dinner and make a few remarks after the meal. Friedman commented that he was delighted to be with us and recalled that he had long known both Mises and Hayek, having himself been one of the founding members of the Mont Pèlerin Society in 1947 when it met for the first time in Switzerland. But what stood out in his remarks for most of us was his statement that there is no such thing as different schools of thought in economics. There is only good economics and bad economics. Clearly, therefore, we were on a fool's errand attending a conference on something called "Austrian" economics.

I doubt one could find many economists who would, in principle, disagree with Friedman's statement. Good economics provides a comprehensive and realistic theoretical understanding of how the world works in terms of such things as human decisionmaking under the constraint of scarcity; the logic of market interactions, including the formation and determination of the prices for finished goods and the factors of production, under conditions of, say, competition, monopoly, or oligopoly; and the social and economic consequences of alternative institutional arrangements, such as capitalism, socialism, or the interventionist–welfare state. Bad economics, on the other hand, fails to do so, either in terms of the theory or evidence presented and therefore in the wrong or incomplete answers to these and a wide variety of other questions.

Of course, every economist considers what he does to be "good" economics and that those whose theoretical and policy views differ from his are doing, well, something less than really "good" economics. Or if that is considered too tactless a manner of putting it in "polite company," then an alternative way of expressing the same thing is to "suggest" that there are some theoretical approaches or questions that are more "interesting" than others.

But in saying this I would not want to create the impression that the vast majority of economists, therefore, think that there are no right answers to economic questions. There may be some economists who are philosophical or epistemological relativists, who sincerely believe there is no objective reality "out there" that needs theoretical and practical understanding and interpretation. But I believe that most economists do accept that reality exists and that the fundamental purpose of any economic theory and its applications is to try to provide some answers to the problems of understanding the real world.

Twenty years ago Dr. James Buchanan delivered an extremely harsh statement about the state of the economics profession as he saw it at the time:

> Economics, as a discipline, became "scientific" over the quarter century, but I put the word in quotation marks and I deliberately use it pejoratively here. As it is practiced in 1983, economics is a science without ultimate purpose or meaning. It has allowed itself to become captive of the technical tools that it employs without keeping track of just what it is that the tools are to be used for. In a very real sense, the economists of the 1980s are illiterate in basic principles of their own discipline. . . . Their motivation is not normative; they seem to be ideological eunuchs. Their interest lies in the purely intellectual properties of the models with which they work, and they seem to get their kicks from the discovery of proofs of propositions relevant only to their own fantasy lands. . . . Our graduate schools are producing highly trained technicians who are blissfully ignorant of the whole purpose of their alleged discipline. They feel no moral obligation to convey and to transmit to their students any understanding of the social process through which a society of free persons can be organized without overt conflict while at the same time using resources with tolerable efficiency.[7]

While there have been significant contributions and additions to our economic knowledge and understanding over the last two decades, I would presume that Dr. Buchanan would still consider the general training and attitude in the economics profession today to be not much different than it was when he wrote these words—only, perhaps, even worse in some respects.

How do we explain this, if what Dr. Buchanan said is basically true? In what ways are many Austrian School economists less guilty of his accusation?

The Ethos of Economic Approaches

I would like to discuss this in terms of the concept of cultural ethos. Culture is often defined as the language, ideas, beliefs, customs, codes, institutions, tools, techniques, works of art, rituals, and ceremonies practiced within a particular society or among a particular people.[8] Ethos is the actual network and content of a group's or a society's guiding beliefs, ideas, customs, institutions, techniques, or modes of expression. Ethos includes the presuppositions that underlie how the members of that group or society see the world. It incorporates attitudes and beliefs about the nature of reality and the way men can know the reality of their world. In intellectual pursuits it specifies the rules of argumentation and justification when members of that group or society attempt to reason with and persuade each other. It establishes the guidelines and rationales concerning what is acceptable as proof of fact and what are the methods for deriving and determining those facts. Ethos also specifies the normative standards and rules for personal and interpersonal conduct and what, therefore, among other things is acceptable and moral behavior.

While it may seem peculiar to apply a concept more likely to be utilized by sociologists or anthropologists, I would suggest that economists as an association of scholars concerned with certain questions surrounding the human condition have their own culture and ethos, too. But just as there is more than one culture in the world with a particular ethos, the same applies within the economics profession. Economics has competing cultures each with it own ethos. On the other hand, I don't want to imply that they exist in splendid isolation. There is constant cross-cultural interaction and trade in ideas and their use. But just as there are some cultures around the world that are "stronger" and more dominating on the global scene, the same applies in the economics profession. Neoclassical, or mainstream, or standard textbook economics is and has been the dominating culture for most of the last one hundred years within the economics profession. And the Austrians have been one of the eclipsed and marginalized alternatives to the neoclassical ethos for most of this time. For the most part, many in the neoclassical tradition have manifested a very common trait in a dominant culture—imperial arrogance. The little societies and cultures are expected to accept the dominant culture's ethos as the standard and benchmark of excellence and right, to which the little societies are expected to conform. Only with reluctance and a tone of condescension do many of the members of the dominant culture give credence to what the other cultures may have to contribute to the enrichment of the human experience.

As a result, those in the smaller or minority cultures tend to learn and absorb far more from the dominant culture than the other way around. Most members of an imperial culture rarely take the time to learn the languages, customs, and histories of those cultures over which they lord. In the economics profession, most Austrian economists acquire a detailed working knowledge of the neoclassical or mainstream approach as part of their academic training and process of professional qualification. Few neoclassical economists have any detailed knowledge of the Austrian approach, and what they do know is often a caricature.

The Ethos of the Austrian School

But having said all this, what are the qualities, characteristics, and features that distinguish the ethos of the Austrian School from that of neoclassical economics? Both are outgrowths of the nineteenth-century classical approach that emerged from the writings of eighteenth-century French Physiocrats and Scottish Moral Philosophers, the most famous of whom were probably Adam Smith and David Hume. These French and Scottish thinkers had uncovered a profoundly important concept: the idea of social and market order without political design. They developed a fairly detailed and systematic understanding of how many, if not most, institutions of society are—as another Scottish scholar, Adam Ferguson, expressed it—the results of human action, but not of human design. Adam Smith ridiculed and warned of the danger from what he called "the man of system," who in his arrogance would presume to know enough to attempt the social engineering of society, regardless of the wishes and knowledge of the social participants about whom he may know nothing and care even less.

The classical economists often referred to a "natural order" in society similar in its independence from arbitrary human control to that discovered in the physical world of physics and chemistry. Man could learn the "laws" of the natural order of society just like he mastered the laws of the physical world. And while he could not defy those laws, once having learned them he could more wisely know what was open to his influence and control for his own purposes—and what was not.[9]

The Austrian School had its beginnings with the publication of Carl Menger's *Grundsatze der Volkswirtschaftslehre* in 1871.[10] He is best known for having formulated a version of the theory of marginal utility, along with the two other founders of the marginalist approach, William Stanley Jevons and Léon Walras. Jevons and Walras structured their variations on the marginalist theme in the garb of mathematical notation, with an emphasis on the conditions and requirements for the existence of equilibrium states.

Menger, on the other hand, presented the theory in a framework that gave greater emphasis to the roles of uncertainty, imperfect knowledge, and causal and time processes of economizing and production. He was more interested in explaining the logic behind the process of price formation, rather than the particulars of a specific equilibrium end-state of affairs in the changing conditions of the market. In addition, he emphasized an aspect of the social process that neither of his two marginalist co-founders gave any serious attention to: the evolution and formation of spontaneous social institutions.[11] Menger's mode of exposition lead Frank H. Knight to comment in 1931 that, "In fact, the entire theory is much more convincing in the loose, common-sense formulation of Menger than it is in the more refined mathematical version of Jevons and Walras."[12]

The Austrian School, however, established its place in the mainstream of economic thought in the 1880s and 1890s through the contributions of Eugen von Böhm-Bawerk[13] and Friedrich von Wieser. The two, who were brothers-in-law, had come across Menger's book when they were students and devoted a good portion of their scholarly efforts over the coming years to develop and extend Menger's ideas. They wrote widely on the topics of value and price, capital and interest, imputation and factor pricing, and opportunity cost. Böhm-Bawerk was the careful methodical logician who assisted in getting Austrian ideas noticed by the economics profession by his willingness

to enter into extensive debates in the pages of the economics journals, both in German and in English. Wieser was more of an introvert
who shied away from debates and argument for the most part, but
attempted to incorporate some of the Austrian ideas within his second field of interest, historical sociology, in which he formulated a
theory of entrepreneurship and leadership for understanding the
nature of social and political processes.[14]

During these first decades of the School's existence, the most
visible battle lines of debate and disagreement seemed to be primarily with the German Historical School. The latter's proponents rejected an essentially logical–deductive approach to economic analysis
for what often appeared an almost purely atheoretical focus on statis-
tical and historical fact gathering from which they believed period-
specific economic "laws" might be derivable. In the wider economics
profession, the "Austrian" approach seemed to many to be merely
one variation on the common marginalist theme. In the 1890s and
1910s, the most heated area of argumentation between Austrians like
Böhm-Bawerk and "neoclassical" economists like John Bates Clark
often seemed to be over "technical" issues of how one should think
about capital and capital goods, that is, as concrete, discrete produced
means of production that are way stations through time leading
to the completion of a finished consumer good (as Böhm-Bawerk
argued), or as a self-sustaining "fund" of capital in which the role of
time and a period of production could be set aside as a not very useful concepts (as Clark insisted).

It is true that below the surface, points of methodological difference were present. Thus, British neoclassical economist Francis Y.
Edgeworth could chide Böhm-Bawerk for missing some nuances in
the logic of price formation because of his failure to construct his
theory in mathematical form.[15] While, in turn, both Böhm-Bawerk
and Wieser could take a young Joseph A. Schumpeter to task for rig-
idly adhering to a mathematical and "positivist" approach that led
him to reason in circles and fail to appreciate the uniquely "mental"
aspects to all economic phenomena and their understanding.[16]

But at this time, in general, these differences in "method" and
"approach" of exposition seemed more a matter of temperament and
training than something central or crucial to the reformulation and

RICHARD M. EBELING   41

development of economic theory on the basis of the marginalist concept. The Austrians began to become more conscious of distinctive features in their approach during the 1920s and, especially, 1930s. In 1932, Hans Mayer, successor to Wieser's chair at the University of Vienna, contrasted what he referred to as the "functional" and "causal-genetic" theories of price. The functional theory, at the core of mathematical school that had grown out of the teachings of Jevons and Walras, focused on a detailed description of *the conditions and requirements for states of general equilibrium.* Mayer also highlighted the distinctly artificial assumptions that were frequently postulated in the formulations of the functional approach. The causal-genetic theory that had emerged from Menger's contributions focused on explaining *the logical processes of price formation out of the interactions of market participants on their basis of their subjective valuations and choices.*[17]

At the same time, in 1931, Ludwig von Mises also argued that "[w]ithin the field of modern economics the Austrian School has shown its superiority to the School of Lausanne and the schools related to the latter, which favor mathematical formulations, by clarifying the causal relationships between value and cost, while at the same time eschewing the concept of function, which in our science is misleading."[18] It was misleading in the social sciences, including economics, Mises had argued earlier in 1929, because it directed attention away from that unique property of the human sciences that is the ultimate causal factor at work that sends the sequence of social events in motion—men's intentional and volitional will. It also gave the false impression that quantitative predictability was possible in the social sciences in the same manner that it was believed possible in the natural sciences. "Economics too can make predictions in the sense in which this ability is attributed to the natural sciences," Mises insisted. "The economist can and does know in advance what effect an increase in the quantity of money will have upon its purchasing power or what consequences price controls must have. . . . However, this knowledge is not quantitatively definite," because it depends upon the subjective valuations, judgments, and expectations of the interacting market participants. And these are always subject to change and modification due to the volitional character of such valuations, judgments, and expectations. Hence, the laws of economics referred to qualitative logical relationships, not quantitative empirical relationships "This is the reason why history cannot predict things to come and why it is an illusion to believe that qualitative economics can be replaced or supplemented by quantitative economics," Mises reasoned. "Economics as a theoretical science can impart no knowledge other than qualitative. And economic history can furnish us with quantitative knowledge only *post factum.*"[19]

It is nonetheless true that what separated the Austrians from the neoclassical economists was not easy to see on the surface, especially following Lionel Robbins's 1932 *Essay on the Nature and Significance of Economic Science,* in which he attempted to synthesize what he saw as the common elements in the Austrian and Lausanne schools in terms of a refined and general conception of the universal logic of human choice under conditions of scarcity.[20] The critical references to and analyses of the mathematical or "functional" approach by Austrians like Mayer and Mises have sometimes confused the issues involved. Neoclassical economists have often presumed that the Austrians were opposed to their method of analysis because of a lack of proper mathematical training or a failure to appreciate the centrality of a careful formalization of the equilibrium concept for any successful economic reasoning. As Austrian economist Ludwig M. Lachmann once observed, "Unfortunately, they [the Austrians] never were able to show, with the cogency their case required, the incompatibility between the idea of planned action, the very core of Austrian economic thought, and an analytical model which knows no action, but only reaction."[21]

The Conception of Choice in
Austrian and Neoclassical Economics

For the neoclassical theorist, man is the "chooser" within a set of superimposed "given" constraints. He is assumed to already have a set of given ends that have been ranked in order of importance, an endowment of given means technologically known to be usable for certain uses and applications, and to be confronted with various terms of trade in the form of market prices at which he may trade off the alternatives amongst which he must choose. Given his tastes, means, and price constraints, the individual merely calculates what has to be the only rational and optimal "choice" in his objectively known circumstances. All the individual's decisions are in principle predictable, in fact, preordained, in this Logic of Choice, since any choice other than the one dictated by the "given" conditions would be by definition suboptimal and therefore contrary to the purpose of utility maximization.

For the Austrians, however, this is beginning the analysis one step removed from its causal origin in the mental processes of the individual actors. The Austrians, in other words, ask from whence come the "givens" the neoclassical approach takes as its starting point? They argue that the individual creatively imagines a future state (or states) of affairs, conceives of ways in which the objects of the world might be usable as means to attain it (or them), tries to discern causal relationships in the use of those means, and weighs the worth to himself of giving up one goal possibly to achieve some other. Thus, "ends," "means," and "trade-offs" arise and are brought into existence from the minds of men; they do not exist independently and separately from the human minds that generate them. This is the basis for the Austrian conception of a wider notion of subjectivism than merely an agent's given tastes and preferences. These intentional activities of the mind are a reason why the Austrians often refer to their approach as a Logic of Action.

The uniqueness of Austrian subjectivism, in contrast to the neoclassical subjectivism of given tastes and preferences, therefore, is its intentionalist starting point. Man is not merely one of many quantitative variables. the simultaneous interactions of which produce a general equilibrium solution. Man, instead, is the focal, the Achimedian, point around which the social world revolves and comes into being. Man is, in the words of the American "Austrian," Frank A. Fetter, not merely the passive evaluator of goods, but the "doer of acts."[22] From Menger through Mises, the Austrians have seen man as the being that gives meaning, order, structure, and significance to the world. Ends and means, costs and benefits, "sooner" or "later" finished consumer goods and factors of production, profit and loss, friend or foe are all ultimately concepts and relationships created by the human mind. The alpha and omega of social phenomena form the subjective world of acting man. The laws of nature and the physical environment may be the limits within which human endeavors are possible of accomplishment, but it is the human actor's conceptions and perceptions of the desirable, possible, and attainable that serve as the driving rod for actions initiated, productions undertaken, and social relationships formed.

This also helps explain why human action and the events of the social world seen far more unpredictable and far less deterministic to the Austrians than they appear to many neoclassical economists. Having assumed the "givenness" of the ends–means structure and the constraints from which any choice will arise, the logic of that choice and its rationality under the circumstances can all be predictively and deterministically explained. Because the decisionmaker saw these as alternative ends from which he would want to or could choose, and that these were the available means and their uses, and given that these were the trade-off options as he saw the possibilities before him, the individual came to—had to come to—the conclusion that "this" was the only logical thing he could—or would—do under the circumstances.

The Austrians see the logic of choice as emerging out of a forward-looking mental process through which an individual *creates in his mind* the elements and options out of which a future choice might arise. From an individual's potential fields of interest, some particular interest (desire, want, "urge," attraction) comes to be the focus of his attention. He imagines some future moment when this interest would be fulfilled if he were to act to bring it about. He pictures what such a state of fulfillment would require. He then mentally brings himself back to the present and imagines ways and means by which he can bring that projected future state of affairs into existence. He may undertake any number of such mental projections into the future, imagining various sets of ends and means that are then competing options vying for accomplishment, and from which he may decide to choose.

He may retrace the mental steps of some previous imagined project to incorporate things he has "learned" and thought of in fantasizing about other imagined projects, and then reshape this earlier goal and plan of action. He begins to compare the alternatives, and thinks what each is worth to him—what is the valued benefit of each and what costs in terms of forgone projects and uses of means he might be willing to pay—as the price to bring any one of them to fruition. All of this takes time. And he cannot be perfectly certain of any outcome.

Herein lies the inherent unpredictability of choice and decision-making in the Logic of Action: The analyst cannot know with predictive certainty what the actor's choice will be ex ante because the actor himself does not know what the alternatives are or how he will evaluate and rank them independent of the temporal "fantasizing" process from which a choice may be made. In this sense, our future choices are not only hidden from the social and economic analyst but from ourselves as well. We can never know our own choices until we make them. Thus knowledge of our own choices is always in our own future, whether that future is a moment from now or decades away.[23]

This is part of the reason behind the Austrian resistance to, and often rejection of, the "mathematical" method in economics. In the neoclassical scheme of things, man is reduced to being one of the "data" in the form of his given tastes and preferences, the quantitative aspect of which now makes its contribution to the determination of general equilibrium outcomes. As Pareto expressed it: "The individual can disappear, provided he leaves us this photograph of his tastes."[24] Man becomes merely one of the dependent variables in a system of interdependent equations for an economic equilibrium. Or, as the Swedish economist Gustav Cassel once stated, man is now "merely fate determined, like wind-blown shavings raised and lowered on the curves of mathematical determination."[25] There is no place in this conception of man for acting men who best know their own interests, or who can best evaluate their own local circumstances, or who can judge how to pursue their own interests and use their local circumstances to the best effect in the face of profit opportunities. Man becomes inanimate matter manifested in the form of relative amounts of various combinations of goods "chosen" when confronted with a "given" set of prices.

Intentionality, Action, and the Market Process

As an extension of this view of man, in general neoclassical economists have been far more receptive to admitting the possibilities for government intervention, regulation, and control than have been the

Austrians. With man viewed as a passive responder to his given circumstances, and with a misplaced confidence on the part of a growing number of economists that they had the ability not only to master qualitatively but quantitatively the interconnected relationships among all factors at work in the economic system, it became in the twentieth century an easy step to conclude that men and their "choices" could be manipulated in the name of attaining more "optimal" outcomes than men left on their own in the market. This attitude was increasingly held by economists on both the "left" and "right." The professional economist possessed the theoretical and quantitative tools to remake, or at least modify, the economic terrain, due to the higher plane from which the neoclassical economist claimed to see the workings of the world.

Many Austrians have, instead, adopted as their conceptual starting point Max Weber's use of the idea of "purposeful action" as human behavior to which "the acting individual attaches a subjective meaning," and "social action" as action by an individual in which he "takes account of the behavior of others and is thereby oriented in its course."[26] In this Weberian framework, individual and intersubjective meanings that the actors assign to their own and the reciprocal conduct of others define the meaning and context of social actions. Thus, according to Weber, an "exchange" is determined by the meanings the actors see in their mutual conduct and "[w]ithout this 'meaning' we are inclined to say that an 'exchange' is neither empirically possible nor conceptually imaginable."[27]

Especially following the writings of Ludwig von Mises, the Austrian economists have argued that a theory of human action should be constructed on the basis of the qualities and characteristics that common-sense reflection suggests are the natural conditions under which the human actor chooses and acts. Thus, the Austrians have emphasized imperfect knowledge, decisionmaking under uncertainty, and the possibility of error. Furthermore, as we have seen, they have argued that "choice" should not be viewed as fully predetermined or predictable from some prior "data" of the "given" situation. Instead, choice emerges from the mental processes in which the actor, in a fundamental sense, creates the "ends" and "means" and the terms of trade in the context of which a choice will be made. Hence, the "givens" of neoclassical theory in which choices are made are, in fact, not given to either actor or analyst prior to the actual choice-making process itself.

The Austrian economists also have assigned crucial importance to understanding the role of the entrepreneur as initiator and coordinator of enterprising activities, and the processes through which multitudes of human plans in the market may or may not be successfully coordinated through the institutions of market competition and the price system.[28] Their emphasis has been less on the final state of any general equilibrium and more on the processes of creation, adjustment, and change in temporal sequences of market interaction. A hypothetical equilibrium state has served more as a conceptual reference point to explain the circumstances under which there would no longer be incentives or opportunities for further profitable actions by either demanders or suppliers. The task of market theory, in the view of most Austrians, has been to logically explain and trace the implications and consequences of the process by which market actors discover potential gains-from-trade at particular moments in time and through time, and initiate actions that take advantage of them.[29]

The Austrian emphasis on active intentionality on the part of individual decisionmakers has led a number of the members of the School to give especial emphasis to the evolution and development of institutions and societal patterns that are the unintended consequences of human action. From the interactions of multitudes of individuals, each pursuing their own particular ends, Austrians such as Menger and Hayek have clarified how a complex social order emerges, forms, and sustains itself, without either prior design or directed central plan. Through evolved rules and codes of interpersonal conduct, and customs and patterns of social and market interaction, individuals may retain a wide latitude of personal freedom in their actions, while, at the same time, constantly having incentives for constructing and adjusting their respective plans in ways that tend to be harmonious with and mutually beneficial for many of the other members of society.[30]

Austrian Economics and Economic Policy

Finally, the Austrians have drawn various economic policy conclusions from their theoretical explorations into social and market phenomena. Their fundamental argument is that a complex economic order cannot successfully function for purposes of mutual coordination of multitudes of human plans without the institutions of private property and market competition. Only in a setting in which individuals may own goods and resources and buy and sell them will they have the incentives and opportunities to evaluate and appraise their usefulness for the attainment of competing purposes to which they could be applied. Out of these valuations and appraisements emerge gains-from-trade that manifest themselves in the form of market prices in consummated transactions. These market prices, expressed in the common denominator of money offered to buy and sell goods and resources, then serve as the device for economic calculation which makes possible the efficient use of the scarce means of production and the economizing of dispersed information for the coordinating of those multitudes of individual consumer and producer plans.

The Austrians concluded that both socialism and political intervention with the free competitive market process prevent or impede effective use of people's abilities and knowledge for the greater mutual benefit of all members of society. Traditional socialism abolishes private property, eliminates private buying and selling of goods and resources, and imposes centrally directed planning on all economic activity. By doing so, socialist central planning does away with the mechanisms for discovering what the members of the society consider worth buying, how best to produce the goods desired by the consuming public, and how to balance the plans of production with those of consumption for a rational apportioning of men and material among their alternative uses.[31]

Political intervention in the market through regulations, controls, and prohibitions does not do away with the competitive process in the same radical manner as comprehensive socialist planning. But it prevents the free choices and decisions of individuals from determining what actually gets produced, in what productive manner, at what prices and costs and for whose mutual benefit. If, as the Austrians have argued, more knowledge is dispersed among the various members of society than can ever be fully mastered, appreciated, and integrated in a single mind or among the best of a handful of minds, then both socialism and political intervention in the market must reduce the effectiveness and efficiency of how the economic order works and its results.[32]

Conclusion

The ethos of the Austrian School, therefore, is grounded in a conception of man and society that attempts to construct a theoretical understanding that takes human beings as they are found in reality. They are men with imperfect knowledge, who choose and act in a world of varying degrees of uncertainty. They are men who give meanings to objects and events, to themselves and others on the basis of their intentions and purposes. They interact with each other in a variety of market settings, but there are no perfect and simultaneous equilibrium solutions under an array of unrealistic assumptions having little do with the natural and human environment in which men pursue opportunities for mutual gains from trade.

Through a process of rivalrous competition and trial and error they discover their potentials and the possibilities for improvement and betterment.[33] In the division of labor there are those who have the specialized role of "entrepreneur," whose task it is to anticipate uncertain future consumer demand, to organize time-consuming production processes, and direct the factors of production employed toward the completion of a finished consumer good, and who may or may not earn profits based on their better reading of the market and the competing actions of their supply-side rivals.

For the Austrians, the notion that those who may man the bureaus, agencies, and departments of government have the knowledge, wisdom, or ability to successfully plan, direct, or regulate the personal and economic affairs of the multitudes in society is nothing short of what Hayek referred to as a "presence of knowledge."[34] Most of the institutions of society, including the rules and standards for order, ethics, and enforcement of agreements, have and continue to evolve outside the narrow arena of political legislation.[35]

The Austrians, therefore, approach the theoretical problems of understanding human society and the policy issues surrounding public affairs with a greater degree of humility and modesty than many others, including a good number of neoclassical economists. They try to be more aware of what men cannot fully acknowledge and totally comprehend when trying to grapple with the course of human events.[36]

In the eyes of many neoclassical economists this seeming lack of precise mathematical determinism, in addition to the Austrian reluctance to reduce men and their affairs to merely manipulatable quantitative dimensions, makes the Austrian School approach to economic analysis appear not to be "rigorous" enough for any claim to the title of being a "real" scientific method.

The Austrian response is to point out that there is much that is imprecise, blurry, and ambiguous in corners of even the most "hard" natural sciences. They also emphasize that the methods and tools of any scientific analysis must be designed to fit the nature and characteristics of the subject matter being investigated. In the arena of man, human meaning and purpose, human plan and action, human memory and expectation represent qualities in the object being studied that cannot be assumed away and for which there are no parallels in the fields of physics or chemistry.[37]

Oskar Morgenstern, one of the co-founders of modern game theory and an economist trained in Vienna by the leading Austrian economists in the period between the two world wars, emphasized the distinct qualities in social phenomena from the subject matter of the physical sciences:

> People are acting sometimes against each other, sometimes cooperatively with each other; they have different degrees of information about each other, their aspirations lead them to conflict or cooperation. Inanimate nature shows none of these traits. Atoms, molecules, stars may coagulate, collide and explode but they do not fight each other; nor do they collaborate. Consequently, it was dubious that the methods and concepts developed in the physical sciences would succeed in being applied to social problems.[38]

The human sciences must take man, with his nature and characteristics, as the measure for constructing a theoretical understanding of human action and the social order and institutions a man's interactions with other men generate through time. Social and market processes of change, adjustment, and coordination are the theater of study, not artificial mathematical imageries of imaginary states of perfect equilibrium.

Humility and not hubris should be the axiom from which economists start their study of man and markets. The Austrians have tried to be more conscious of this. The relevancy and greater realism of the Austrian approach suggest the benefits of rarely losing sight of this starting point in their research and writings.

Notes

[1] For an exposition and a contrast of the Austrian and Keynesian explanations of and policy prescriptions for the Great Depression of the 1930s, see Richard M. Ebeling, "The Austrian Economists and the Keynesian Revolution: The Great Depression and the Economics of the Short-Run," in Richard M. Ebeling, ed., *Human Action: A 50-Year Tribute* (Hillsdale, MI: Hillsdale College Press, 2000), pp. 15–110

[2] For a presentation of the many of the theoretical and policy themes in the writings of the Austrian economists, see Richard M. Ebeling, "The Significance of Austrian Economics in 20th Century Economic Thought," in *Austrian Economics and the Political Economy of Freedom* (Northampton, MA: Edward Elgar, 2003), pp. 34–60; also Ludwig M. Lachmann, "The Significance of the Austrian School of Economics in the History of Ideas" [1966], reprinted in Richard M. Ebeling, ed., *Austrian Economics: A Reader* (Hillsdale, MI: Hillsdale College Press, 1990), pp. 17–39.

[3] For an overview of Mises' contributions to economic theory and policy, see Richard M. Ebeling, "A Rational Economist in an Irrational Age: Ludwig von Mises," in *Austrian Economics and the Political Economy of Freedom*, pp. 61–100.

[4] For a summary of Hayek's life and contributions to economics, see Richard M. Ebeling, "Friedrich A. Hayek: A Centenary Appreciation," *The Freeman* (May 1999): 28–32.

[5] For a summary of Kirzner's contributions to Austrian economics, see Richard M. Ebeling, "Israel M. Kirzner and the Austrian Theory of Competition and Entrepreneurship," *Freedom Daily* (August 2001): 8–14.

[6] The lectures delivered by Kirzner, Rothbard, and Lachmann were later published in Edwin G. Dolan, ed., *The Foundations of Modern Austrian Economics* (Kansas City: Sheed & Ward, 1976).

[7] James M. Buchanan, "Political Economy: 1957–1982" in *Liberty, Market, and State: Political Economy in the 1980s* (New York: New York University Press, 1985), pp. 14–15.

[8] "Culture." *Encyclopedia Britannica*, 2003. Encyclopedia Britannica Premium Service. 03 Feb 2003. <http://www.britannica.com/eb/article?eu=118246>.

[9]On the contributions of the classical economists and their differences from modern neoclassical economics, see Richard M. Ebeling, "How Economics Became the Dismal Science: The Classical Economists and 20th Century Economics," in *Austrian Economics and the Political Economy of Freedom*, pp. 1–13.

[10]Carl Menger, *Principles of Economics* [1871] (New York: New York University Press, 1981).

[11]Carl Menger, *Investigations into the Methods of the Social Sciences with Special Reference to Economics* [1884] (New York: New York University Press, 1985), pp. 139–59.

[12]Frank H. Knight, "Marginal Utility" [1931], reprinted in *The Ethics of Competition* (New York: Harper & Brothers, 1935), p. 160.

[13]For a brief summary of Böhm-Bawerk's life and contributions, see Richard M. Ebeling, "Eugen von Böhm-Bawerk: A Sesquicentennial Appreciation," *Ideas on Liberty* (February 2001), pp. 36–41.

[14]Friedrich von Wieser, *The Law of Power* [1926] (Lincoln, NE: Bureau of Business Research, 1983).

[15]Francis Y. Edgeworth, "Professor Böhm-Bawerk on the Ultimate Standard of Value" [1892], reprinted in *Papers Relating to Political Economy*, Vol. III (London: Macmillan, 1925), pp. 59–64.

[16]Eugen von Böhm-Bawerk, *Capital and Interest*, Vol. 3 (South Holland, IL: Libertarian Press), pp. 228–29; and Friedrich von Wieser, "The Nature and Substance of Theoretical Economics" [1911], in Israel M. Kirzner, ed., *Classics in Austrian Economics*, Vol. I (London: William Pickering, 1994), pp. 285–303.

[17]Hans Mayer, "The Cognitive Value of Functional Theories of Price" [1932], in Israel M. Kirzner, ed., *Classics of Austrian Economics*, Vol. II (London: William Pickering, 1994), pp. 55–168

[18]Ludwig von Mises, "On the Development of the Subjective Theory of Value" [1931], in *Epistemological Problems of Economics* [1933] (New York: New York University Press, 1981), p. 165; attention has been drawn to Mises' comment the following year, in 1932, at a meeting of the *Verein fur Sozialpolitik* in Dresden, Germany ("The Controversy Over the Theory of Value" [1932], ibid., p. 214), that "Within modern subjectivist economics it has become customary to distinguish several schools. We usually speak of the Austrian School and the Anglo-American Schools and the School of Lausanne. . . . [T]hese three schools of thought differ only in their mode of expressing the same fundamental idea and that they are divided more by their terminology and by peculiarities of presentation than by the substance of their teachings," to suggest that Mises did not at this time really and fully see the difference between the Austrian and neoclassical approaches. But considering his comment the year before, in 1931, a more reasonable interpretation is that at the meeting of the *Verein* he was emphasizing to an audience made up of a large number of Marxists and members of the German Historical School that the great divide was between all those who understood the logic of the laws of economics along "marginalist" lines regardless of the difference in approaches, and those either like the

Marxists who still adhered to the classical labor theory of value or the German Historicists who rejected any universal and theoretical laws of economics.

[19]Mises, "Sociology and History" [1929], ibid., pp. 116–18.

[20]Lionel Robbins, *An Essay on the Nature and Significance of Economic Science* [1932] (London: Macmillan, rev. ed., 1935).

[21]Ludwig M. Lachmann, "Methodological Individualism and the Market Economy," [1969] in Walter E. Grinder, ed., *Capital, Expectations, and the Market Process: Essays on the Theory of the Market Economy* (Kansas City: Sheed Andrews and McMeel, 1977), p. 164, n.9.

[22]Frank A. Fetter, *Economic Principles* (New York: The Century Co., 1915), pp. 171–72.

[23]I have attempted to develop some aspects of this intentionalist approach and a complementary Austrian theory of expectations-formation in the market process, see Richard M. Ebeling "Human Action, Ideal Types, and the Market Process; Alfred Schutz and the Austrian Economists," in Lester Embree, ed., *Schutzian Social Science* (Norwell, MA: Kluwer Academic Publishers, 1999), pp. 115–34; "Austrian Subjectivism and Phenomenological Foundations" in Peter J. Boettke and Mario J. Rizzo, eds., *Advances in Austrian Economics,* Vol. 2 (part A) (Greenwich, CT: JAI Press, 1995), pp. 39–53; "Expectations and Expectations-Formation in Mises' Theory of the Market Process," in Peter J. Boettke and David L. Prychitko, eds., *The Market Process: Essays in Contemporary Austrian Economics* (Brookfield, VT: Edward Elgar, 1994), pp. 83–95; "Cooperation in Anonymity" and "Toward a Hermeneutical Economics: Expectations, Prices, and the Role of Interpretation in a Theory of the Market Process," in David L. Prychitko, ed., *Individuals, Institutions, Interpretations: Hermeneutics Applied to Economics* (Brookfield, VT: Edward Elgar, 1995), pp. 81–92 & 138–53; and "What is a Price? Explanation and Understanding" in Don Lavoie, ed,, *Economics and Hermeneutics* (London/New York: Routledge, 1990), pp. 177–94.

[24]Vilfredo Pareto, *Manual of Political Economy* [1927] (New York: Augustus M. Kelley 1971), p. 120.

[25]Quoted in Eric Englund, "Gustav Cassel's Autobiography," *Quarterly Journal of Economics* (May 1943): 474.

[26]Max Weber, *The Theory of Social and Economic Organization* (New York: Oxford University Press, 1947), p. 88.

[27]Max Weber, *Critique of Stammler* (New York: Free Press, 1977), p. 112.

[28]Ludwig von Mises, *Human Action, A Treatise on Economics* [1949] (Irvington-on-Hudson, NY: Foundation for Economic Education, 4th rev. ed., 1996), pp. 257–397; Israel M. Kirzner, *Competition and Entrepreneurship* (Chicago: University of Chicago Press, 1973), and "The Primacy of Entrepreneurial Discovery" [1980] reprinted in Richard M. Ebeling, ed., *Austrian Economics: A Reader* (Hillsdale, MI: Hillsdale College Press, 1990), pp. 304–33.

[29]Mises, *Human Action*, pp. 236–56.

[30]Friedrich A. Hayek, *The Counter-Revolution of Science* [1952] (Indianapolis, IN: Liberty Fund, 1987); "The Results of Human Action but not of Human Design" [1967] in *Studies in Philosophy, Politics and Economics* (Chicago: University of Chicago Press, 1967), pp. 96–105; *Law, Legislation and Liberty,* Vol. 1: "Rules and Order" (Chicago: University of Chicago Press, 1973); also see Anthony Flew, *Thinking about Social Thinking: The Philosophy of the Social Sciences* (New York: Blackwell, 1985), pp. 54–80.

[31]See Richard M. Ebeling, "Economic Calculation Under Socialism: Ludwig von Mises and His Predecessors," in *Austrian Economics and the Political Economy of Freedom* (Northampton, MA: Edward Elgar, 2003), pp. 101–35.

[32]See Richard M. Ebeling, "The Free Market and the Interventionist State: The Political Economy of Public Policy" in *Austrian Economics and the Political Economy of Freedom*; I have explained the development and content of Ludwig von Mises' various policy writings in Austria during the years 1918–1938, when he was a senior policy analyst for the Vienna Chamber of Commerce; see Richard M. Ebeling, "The Economist as the Historian of Decline: Ludwig von Mises and Austria Between the Two World Wars" in Richard M. Ebeling, ed., *Globalization: Will Freedom or World Government Dominate the International Marketplace?* (Hillsdale, MI: Hillsdale College Press, 2002), pp. 1–68; and I have explained Mises' ideas concerning post-World War II European economic reform and reconstruction in the context of his general system of ideas in Richard M. Ebeling, "Planning for Freedom: Ludwig von Mises as Political Economist and Policy Analyst," in Richard M. Ebeling, ed., *Competition or Compulsion? The Market Economy versus the New Social Engineering* (Hillsdale, MI: Hillsdale College Press, 2001), pp. 1–85. I have also discussed the Austrian theory of money, monetary policy, and the business cycle in the context of the Great Depression and in contrast to Keynesian Economics, and in comparison to the ideas of Joseph Schumpeter in Richard M. Ebeling, "The Austrian Economists and the Keynesian Revolution: The Great Depression and the Economics of the Short-Run," and "Two Variations on the Austrian Monetary Theme: Ludwig von Mises and Joseph A. Schumpeter on the Business Cycle" in Richard M. Ebeling, ed., *Human Action: A 50-Year Tribute* (Hillsdale, MI: Hillsdale College Press, 2000), pp. 15–110 & 149–87. For a comparison of the similarities and differences between the Austrian and the Swedish economists on money, monetary policy, and business cycle, see Richard M. Ebeling, "Money, Economic Fluctuations, Expectations and Period Analysis: The Austrian and Swedish Economists in the Interwar Period," in Willem Keizer, Bert Tieben, and Rudy van Zip, eds., *Austrian Economics in Debate* (London/New York: Routledge, 1997), pp. 42–74; and for a contrast of the views of the Austrians and the German liberal economists, see Richard M. Ebeling, "The Limits of Economic Policy: The Austrian Economists and the German ORDO Liberals" in *Austrian Economics and the Political Economy of Freedom*, pp. 231–46.

[33]See Friedrich A. Hayek, "Competition as a Discovery Procedure" [1969] in *New Studies in Philosophy, Politics, Economics and the History of Ideas* (Chicago: University of Chicago Press, 1978), pp. 179–90; and "The Meaning of Competition" [1946] reprinted in Richard M. Ebeling, ed., *Austrian Economics: A Reader*, pp. 264–80.

[34]Friedrich A. Hayek, "The Presence of Knowledge," [1974] in *New Studies in Philosophy, Politics, Economics and the History of Ideas*, pp. 23–34.

[35]Friedrich A. Hayek, "The Errors of Constructivism," [1970] in *New Studies in Philosophy, Politics, Economics and the History of Ideas*, pp. 3–22; also see John Blundell and Colin Robinson, *Regulation Without the State. . . . The Debate Continues* (London: Institute of Economic Affairs, 2000); and, Richard M. Ebeling, "The Market Economy and the Political Process: Self-Government, Bureaucracy, and Interventionism," in Richard M. Ebeling, ed., *Free Markets or Bureaucracy? Economic Problem-Solving in the 21st Century* (Hillsdale, MI: Hillsdale College Press, 2003), pp. 1–27.

[36]Friedrich von Wieser, *Social Economics* [1914] (New York: Augustus M. Kelley, 1967), p. 162: "How could any contractual agreement be reached as to institutions whose being is still hidden in the mists of the future, and is only conceived in an incomplete manner by a few far-seeing persons, while the great mass can never clearly appreciate the nature of such an institution until it has actually attained its full form and is generally operative?"

[37]See Fritz Machlup, "If Matter Could Talk," [1969] in *Methodology of Economics and Other Social Sciences* (New York: Academic Press, 1978), pp. 309–32.

[38]Oskar Morgenstern, "Foreword" to Morton D. Davis, *Game Theory: A Nontechnical Introduction* (New York: Basic Books, 1970), p. x.

JOSHUA MURAVCHIK

The Rise and Fall of Socialism

Much of the history of the last two centuries has revolved around the pursuit of a single idea—socialism. It has been the most popular political idea man has ever invented. In some ways, even the great religions cannot compare. Christianity, the most widely embraced religion in history, today claims adherence by one-third of the human race, a proportion reached about a century ago, in other words, after 1,900 years. It took Christianity 300 years before it could claim to speak for 10 percent of the world's people. By comparison, within 150 years after the term "socialism" was coined, roughly 60 percent of the human race found itself living under socialist rule of one kind or another.

Of course, not all who lived under socialism adhered to it philosophically, but vast numbers did. No other political belief claimed the allegiance of so many voters or party members. Nor was there any in which so much energy and hope was invested.

The story of socialism began in the French revolution. The rights it first proclaimed—"liberty, property, security"—closely resembled the American triad of "life, liberty, and the pursuit of happiness." However, soon a fourth was added—equality. To be sure, the Americans had proclaimed that men were "created equal," but the French innovation was to include "equality" among the mandatory pursuits of government. "Equality" was no longer simply a moral value that needed to be asserted but a condition of life that needed to be fos-

---

A Bradley Lecture delivered at the American Enterprise Institute, February 8, 1999.

tered. The revolutionaries added still another objective, brotherhood, so that the enduring slogan of the Revolution became "liberty, equality, brotherhood."

The first to see that the way to give shape to this stirring but vague slogan was through socialism—to wit, the substitution of common ownership for private property—was a revolutionist from Picardy named François-Noel "Gracchus" Babeuf.

There had been earlier thinkers—Rousseau, Thomas More, Plato —whose ideas were in some sense socialist, but it was the French Revolution, and specifically Babeuf, who transformed socialism from a speculative fancy into a fighting creed.

In 1796, Babeuf organized the "conspiracy of equals." The "equals" advocated a system "depriving every individual of the hope of ever becoming either richer, or more powerful, or more outstanding through his learning, than any [other]." They recognized that this would not be easy to achieve. "The sole means," they said, would be "to abolish private property; to have each man . . . deposit the fruit [of his labor] in a common storehouse; and to set up a simple distributing agency, . . . which . . . will allocate the [goods] with the most scrupulous equality."[1]

Babeuf counted himself a thorough democrat, denouncing the use of property qualifications for political functions. But he confronted a dilemma that was to plague socialists often: The people were not ready to follow him. They had been misled. "Thanks to the horrible cunning of the Patriciate," he wrote, "a handful of constant and energetic republicans," namely he and his confreres, found themselves opposed by "a coalition" consisting of not only " the government," and "the well-to-do," but also "the multitude." Thus his band would be compelled to establish a dictatorship "until this new revolution shall be consolidated" and "the level of opinion will be raised"[2]—or as we would say today, the people's consciousness will be raised. Before they could launch their insurrection, Babeuf and his fellow conspirators were arrested, tried, and punished. Babeuf was guillotined.

It was not until a generation later that a new group of socialists emerged, this time in England as well as France. They are known to us as "the utopians," a sobriquet attached to them by Marx and Engels. It was they who coined the term "socialism." Whereas Babeuf had hoped to seize power violently and impose his system on the

whole nation, the utopians set about to teach by example. Their method was to create model communities, the happiness of which would
so impress mankind as to inspire general emulation.

The most fruitful of the utopians were Britain's Robert Owen and
France's Charles Fourier. Both looked to the virgin soil of America as
the natural ground on which to erect their experimental societies. Indeed, the New World extended an idealistic embrace to these innova-
tors. Owen arrived in the United States late in 1824 and before long
was invited to address the House of Representatives. Both President
Monroe and President-elect John Quincy Adams sat in the chamber
to hear him.

A few months later the "Preliminary Society of New Harmony"
was founded by Owen and some 800 to 900 followers. It was located on
the Wabash River in Indiana on a tract of land purchased from George
Rapp and his followers, a Lutheran sect that had successfully developed it over the previous decade into one of the most prosperous communities in the West. A letter by William Shephard, a neighbor who
handled the continuing financial transactions between Rapp and Owen,
described the transformation in evidence within a year after the Owen-
ites took over: "The comfortable gardens, and vines which used to
spread and twine about the older habitations, generally gone to ruin.
The gardens mostly full of weeds (not full of usefull vegetables as formerly) and in many instances the fences broken down and completely
open to the streets—a general carelessness seems to prevail; I have
seen cows and hogs grazing in some of the gardens and grounds."[3]

Within two years New Harmony collapsed entirely. The brevity
of New Harmony was hardly atypical of the experimental socialist
communities. Fourier's communities were called "phalanxes." In Fourier's design, not only would all members of the community be entitled to an economic "social minimum," but also to an assured "sexual
minimum" since "the sexual needs of men and women can become
just as urgent as their need for food."[4] Perhaps due to the promise of
the provision of sexual as well as material needs, Fourierist phalanxes
sprung up in even greater profusion than Owenite villages, but there
were many of each. Their median life span was two years.

Had socialism remained the province of adventurers like Babeuf
and visionaries like Owen and Fourier it might never have constitut-

ed more than a footnote to history. But then it was taken up and transformed by the mightiest secular prophet who ever lived.

Karl Marx disdained the utopians as so many "organizers of charity, members of societies for the prevention of cruelty to animals, temperance fanatics, hole-and-corner reformers of every imaginable kind."[5] In contrast, he offered "scientific socialism." This was a spectacular inversion. What is science but the practice of experimentation, of hypothesis and test? Owen and Fourier and their followers were the real "scientific socialists." They hit upon the idea of socialism, and they tested it by attempting to form socialist communities. In all, there were scores of these tests in America and England—and all of them failed, utterly and disastrously.

Then Marx came along and said never mind these experiments at bringing about socialism by human devices, it will be brought about by the impersonal force of history. In other words, under the banner of "science," Marx shifted the basis for socialism from human ingenuity to sheer prophecy.

The Marxist historian Hobsbawm wrote that "it was not until Karl Marx . . . transferred the centre of gravity of the argument for socialism from its rationality or desirability to its historic inevitability that socialism acquired its most formidable intellectual weapon."[6] Logically, the discovery that socialism was inevitable should have had the effect of bringing an end to the active quest for it. Why strive to achieve what must happen anyway? But it had the opposite effect, including on Marx himself, who devoted his life to the struggle.

He took the lead in founding the International Workingman's Association in 1864, but eight years later, frustrated by the refusal of various affiliated parties to follow his dictates, Marx consigned the organization to oblivion by having its headquarters transferred to Philadelphia.

While Marx's activism was fruitless, his prophecy was fertile. Socialist parties sprang up all over Europe with the growth of parliamentary institutions and of industry, and in 1889, six years after Marx's death, they came together to form the so-called Second International. The ensuing twenty-five years—until World War I—constituted what Leszek Kolakowski has called "the golden age of Marxism."[7]

Ironically, however, the core of Marx's theory was already crumbling. Instead of growing poorer, the workers in industrialized countries were experiencing an improvement in their standards of living, and the middle class, instead of disappearing, was expanding. In the interval between the publication of the *Communist Manifesto* and the founding of the Second International real per capita income in the major European countries nearly doubled.

These developments not only weakened the original rationale for socialism, they also undermined Marx's prediction that the working class would come to the conclusion that it must overthrow the system. If the workers could improve their lot under capitalism, then why turn to revolution? Indeed, half a century after Marx thought he had solved the problem of how socialism would come about, the proletariat showed little sign of playing its appointed role.

This disappointment impressed itself on the two most fertile socialist minds of the day, Eduard Bernstein and Vladimir Ulyanov, who called himself Lenin. Bernstein's solution was to continue to use the label "socialist" but to abandon the goal of socialism. " I cannot believe in a final aim of socialism," he said. "But I strongly believe in the socialist movement, in the march forward of the working classes."[8] Lenin, on the other hand, clung to the goal of socialism but gave up on the working class in favor of a "genuine vanguard" of "people who make revolutionary activity their profession."[9]

Then World War I delivered the coup de grace to Marxism. A key tenet was that "the working men have no country." This was not merely an expression of alienation. It was a corollary of the premise that class is the fundamental political variable. Yet when world war came, the majority of socialists on all sides put country ahead of class. Nonetheless it turned out that the life of socialism, indeed of Marxism, was scarcely begun. As Marx had rescued socialism from the failure of the experiments of the so-called utopians, so now Lenin rescued Marxism from the failure of major parts of its prophecy.

Whether the coup that Lenin pulled off in October 1917 was either "socialist" or a "revolution," properly speaking, has been disputed. But as far as most of the world was concerned, a socialist revolution had come to Russia. However much violence was done to Marxist doctrine in the process, this event furnished Marxism with its most compelling validation: Its teleology was confirmed. Until then, socialism was only a banner, a platform. Now it was in power in one of the largest nations in the world. Here was the proof that history was indeed headed in a direction that put capitalism at its back and socialism in its future. This assurance buttressed even those schools of socialism that had rejected the Soviet model.

Lenin later said that wresting power from the weak and scrupulous provisional government had been as easy as "picking up a feather." Destroying "capitalism" was also easy. People could be shot for exchanging goods in the market, and shot they were. But building "socialism" was more difficult. For six years Lenin labored at it until the exertion killed him. Still, despite failing to create anything that resembled the abstract model of socialism domestically, the U.S.S.R. achieved dramatic results internationally. Either by conquest or by nurturing local communists, it succeeded in spreading regimes modeled after itself over one-third of the world's population. In addition, Lenin's model inspired emulation in the form of Fascism and Nazism.

Benito Mussolini was raised in a Red household where his father used to read to the family from *Das Kapital*. (Parents who have trouble putting the kids to sleep might take note.) Mussolini rose rapidly in the ranks of the Italian Socialist Party. When he decided to support Italy's entry into World War I, he left the party to join other pro-war socialists who took as their symbol the fasces that had been a symbol of Revolutionary France. This did not prevent Mussolini from continuing to call himself a socialist as late as 1920, two years before seizing power, and continuing to campaign for nationalization of the land, workers' participation in the running of factories, and partial expropriation of capital.

Like Mussolini, Hitler studied and admired Lenin. Hitler, too, developed his own unique ideology, and not in name alone were the socialist roots of National Socialism visible. Upon taking power, Hitler made May Day—the international socialist holiday—a national holiday. Nazi authorities commissioned statues, reminiscent of Soviet "socialist realism," glorifying heavily muscled laborers. They developed the "people's car," the *Volkswagen*. And they incanted the slogan, "equality of all racial Germans."

If Fascism and Nazism were metastasized forms of socialism, socialism spread in benign forms, as well. The most important was social democracy, which pursued peaceful and piecemeal reform. But it would be an exaggeration to say that Bernstein's views prevailed. Moderate though they were in action, most social democrats did not accept Bernstein's idea that "the final aim is nothing."[10] Rather, they believed that the final aim could be reached gradually and democratically.

After World War II, new varieties of socialism were created in the newly independent states of Africa, Arabia, and elsewhere. In all some fifty to sixty third world countries went down this path, not counting those like Cuba or Vietnam that adopted more standard communist systems. By the mid- or late 1970s, socialism—either in its communist, social democratic, or third world forms—held sway over 60 percent of the world.

Yet behind the surface of these dazzling political successes, socialism was suffering two critical failures. The first was its inability to sink roots in America. The history of socialism in American consists of European socialists immigrating and setting up socialist parties, clubs, and newspapers—only to have their own convictions or those of their children dissolved in the American atmosphere of freedom and social mobility.

America itself did not embody a formal ideology but it offered a model. It showed the world a system of prosperity, opportunity, and civic equality, or, to put it more simply, a society in which the good life was available to the common man. Although lacking in theoretical paraphernalia, the American way presented an alternative to socialism.

America's success underscored socialism's other critical failure, and that was its own economic performance. The more that socialism was implemented, the worse things got. Even with socialism at its apogee, leaders in disparate corners of the earth were groping for paths by which their societies could escape the cul de sacs into which socialism had led them. The two who launched the worldwide about-face were an odd couple: China's Deng Xiaoping and England's Margaret Thatcher. In 1978, at the party's Third Plenum, Deng announced China's "second revolution."

The "modernization" of agriculture rested upon a resurrection of private farming which was gradually expanded and extended into other spheres. The goal was not to create a market economy, but to move China forward. As Deng explained: "After years of practice it turned out that the old stuff didn't work." They called the new stuff "socialism with Chinese characteristics," but every day it bore greater

resemblance to capitalism. The hard-of-hearing Deng himself obliquely confessed: "Marx sits up in heaven. . . . He sees what we are doing,
and he doesn't like it. So he has punished me by making me deaf."[11]

Within a year of the Plenum at which Deng launched his "second
revolution," Britain began its own "modernizations" with the election
of Thatcher. Unlike previous Conservative administrations, Thatcher
set out to "kill" socialism, which she believed was the true cause of the
so-called "British disease," which others saw as a mysterious and irre-
mediable decline of national culture She was so successful that when
the Labour Party regained power in 1996 Tony Blair declared: "I believe passionately that our government will fail if it sees its task as dis-
mantling Thatcherism. We can't just switch the clock back."[12]

If Thatcher's harsh judgment of democratic socialism was vali-
dated by the success of her policies, it was reconfirmed by complementary events across the English Channel. In France in 1981, the
Socialist Party, led by François Mitterand, scored an electoral victory
of historic proportions. At once it began to implement measures creating new public sector jobs, nationalizing industries, and mandating
increases in wages, pensions, and welfare.

Within a year the economy was in such a tailspin that Mitterand
ordered an abrupt reversal. "The aim is to bring about a real reconciliation between the left and the economy," explained Lionel Jospin,
who was then the general secretary of the Socialist Party, and later
prime minister.[13] The French, like other European social democrats,
recognized that socialism could be a kind of tax upon capitalism, but
it could not be an alternative. Today the debate is about the limits of
that tax.

The capitulation of the West European social democrats and
the free market reforms in China were both momentous changes,
but they were soon to be eclipsed by an even more dramatic chapter
in the history of socialism: the crumbling of the Soviet Union. In
addition to precipitating a flight from socialism in the nations that
had been under Moscow's rule, the Soviet collapse reverberated
throughout the third world. The most profound impact was felt in
Africa, the principle redoubt of third world socialism. Of the thirty-
four African countries that had once embraced socialism, by the early
1990s all but a handful had renounced it. Even Julius Nyerere, once the

avatar of African socialism, confessed: "If I call back the British to look at their old plantations, they will laugh at us because we ruined them."[14]

In Nyerere's Tanzania and all around the world nations attempted to escape the wreckage of socialism. But in some ways the most telling episode in the global flight from socialism was not an escape from failure but from success. In Israel, dedicated Zionist pioneers struggling to recreate a nation in the most inhospitable of human and natural environments had built pure socialist communities called *kibbutzim*. In them, things were owned in common, children were raised communally, decisions were reached democratically, and economic arrangements attained to Marx's formula "from each according to his ability, to each according to his needs." The *kibbutzim* played a critical part in the establishment of the Jewish state.

Yet by the 1980s, population began to flow away from the *kibbutzim*, and even the stalwarts who remained began to shed, a layer at a time, their socialist practices.

The *kibbutzim* constituted but a small part of a small country. Nonetheless, their decline makes for a terribly poignant ending to the story of socialism. In scores of countries over many decades, people strove to bring socialism into being. Again and again they failed. Some of the failures were attributed to unpropitious conditions, others to weak human material, or to coercive methods, or to the stranglehold of the international financial markets. But the *kibbutzim* surmounted all such obstacles. There, at last, living, breathing socialism true to the ideal was built. And when this promised land was reached, it turned out to be an unsatisfying place to live, although there was milk and honey. In the end, socialism was a case of "build it and they will leave."

This ironic denouement would make the story of socialism a nice little vignette in the human comedy were it not for the devastating price that was paid. Communism took a toll of one hundred million or more lives, not to mention all of the other misery engendered. But isn't communism an aberrant form of socialism, a perversion of a great humanitarian ideal? In describing Lenin, I have already explained what made his emendation of Marxism necessary, but an examination of the thoughts and actions of the earliest socialists leads to the conclusion that far from being an aberration, the totalitarian impulse in socialism was there from the beginning.

Babeuf and his comrades knew that they could not cede power to the people until their consciousness had been raised. To this end they foresaw that it would be "of sovereign importance to the cause of equality to keep the citizens incessantly exercised—to attach them to their country, by making them love its ceremonies, its games, its amusements."[15] They planned show trials for "enemies of the people." And they anticipated many of the other features we associate with twentieth-century communism, including driving the population out of the cities, which they saw as dens of bourgeois decadence, back to the honest work of the countryside, a goal realized 180 years later by the Khmer Rouge.

The good-hearted Robert Owen ran New Harmony, and a later similar venture in Britain called Queenstown, as a dictator. At his famous mills at New Lanark, Scotland, each employee's behavior was ranked daily on a scale of 1 to 4, the ranking displayed prominently above his workstation and recorded in a permanent record book. There, too, neighborhood committees were organized to inspect and record the cleanliness of each household. Derisively referred to as "bug-hunters" by the housewives, they foreshadowed the block committees by which Fidel Castro and Nicaragua's Sandinistas exerted social control.

Even Edward Bellamy, whose 1887 novel, *Looking Backward*, constituted a highpoint in the popularity of socialist ideas in America, and who was free to create his socialist society however he liked since he was building it only in a work of fiction, created a chilling image. All laborers were first to be sent for three years to "a very strict [school] in which the young men are taught habits of obedience, subordination and devotion to duty."[16] After that, any slackers are put in solitary confinement on bread and water.

In light of these beginnings, not to mention Marx's denigration of bourgeois democracy, his vituperation toward those who disagreed with him, and his own authoritarian manner, we are on stronger ground to say that it is the social democrats who constitute the aberration of socialism.

To the toll exacted by communism we must add that of third world socialism, which, in addition to countless episodes of brutality, wrecked the chance of progress for a full generation or more throughout the world's poorest lands. The human price of this no one has attempted to tally.

As for the social democratic and labor parties of Europe, while none produced socialism, neither did they produce mass death. They cushioned the bumps in the progress of free economies in exchange for a price in economic efficiency, which at its extreme had a stultifying effect. There is, however, one heavier item to be weighed in assessing the costs of European socialism. That is Fascism and Nazism, which took tens of millions of lives. I have already described the socialist roots of Fascism and Nazism. It remains to be added that they arose in a European culture in which bourgeois society had been systematically discredited by the enchantment of socialism, which characterized it as doomed to be replaced by a new and glorious epoch. This was the incubator that hatched Italian and German Fascism just as it hatched Russian and Chinese communism.

In sum, socialism proved to be mankind's greatest mistake since the serpent beguiled Eve. What was so beguiling about socialism?

Clemenceau said that any man who is not a socialist at twenty has no heart and any man who is still a socialist at forty has no brain. A person at twenty might see that there are poor and there are rich, and the discrepancy can be painful. At twenty, knowing more about consuming than producing, he might assume that the poor are poor because the rich are rich, as if goods exist in given quantities and the main issue is how to distribute them. But sometime between twenty and forty he will probably learn that the amount of privation—in the world or in a society—is far more dependent on variations in the production of wealth than in its distribution and, moreover, that insofar as policy aims to control the distribution it runs the risk of impeding production. In other words, that there is no escape from inequality, except through uniform poverty. Contrary to Clemenceau, however, socialism has appealed far more than just to twenty-year-olds. To understand its remarkable attraction we must look beyond economic innocence.

Although socialism spoke a lot about economics, its appeal lay deeper. Babeuf and his comrades insisted on absolute equality because they believed it was essential to brotherhood. Socialism touched man's pained sense of distance from fellow man, proposing to create an unprecedented bondedness among diverse individuals. Bellamy said the key to socialism is that "the brotherhood of man" would become "as real and vital as physical fraternity."[17] But this, too, is a jejune ideal as Aristotle recognized in critiquing Plato's suggestion of raising children in common: "[W]e might say that each citizen has a thousand sons but . . . no person will concern himself very much about any of them. . . . Anybody would rather have a cousin who really was his cousin than a son shared in the manner described."[18] Moreover, as the *kibbutz* experience has shown, people simply do not want to be that deeply involved in other people's lives nor do they wish to have others that involved in theirs. Humans do have a need for sociality, but they also have a need for privacy, or, as pop psychology puts it, for "space."

Judaism and Christianity tell us that people are brothers insofar as we are all children of G–d. But the Bible also tells us that brotherhood in and of itself does not assure closeness or kindness. The first brothers were Cain and Abel; soon came Jacob and Esau; then Joseph and his brethren. Rather, in this view, it is by striving for closeness to G–d that people are most likely to achieve some measure of meaningful brotherliness with their fellow man. The Bible also recognizes the sometimes painful facts of human inequality, and it speaks to them. It sternly enjoins protection of the widow, the orphan, the blind, the lame. It orders constant charity to the poor. It commands us not to covet. On the issue of inequality, as on the issue of brotherhood, Judaeo-Christian tradition teaches that perfect solutions are not to be found in this world. Instead it offers transcendence, man's path to which lies through righteousness and good deeds.

Socialists have, however, in the main, militantly opposed the biblical religions. The French Revolution created a new calendar commencing with the overthrow of the monarchy instead of the birth of Christ. Babeuf's comrade Sylvain Marechal, author of the *Manifesto of the Equals,* was also the author of *The Atheist's Dictionary;* he used to call himself l'HSD (*l'Homme Sans Dieu*). Owen once said: "There is no sacrifice I would not have made had I been able to terminate the existence of religion on earth."[19] Marx's view of religion is well-known.

This is not to say, however, that socialists have been austere rationalists. On the contrary, the French Revolution offered its own deist substitute for Christianity. Owen became a spiritualist and held daily seances with the departed, even producing in this manner a couple of posthumous works by Shakespeare. Engels wrote the first two drafts of the *Communist Manifesto*, calling them the communist's *Confession of Faith* until Marx changed the title. Marx, as I have said, offered sheer prophecy in the imposture of science, which prophecy, Hobsbawm let slip, was socialism's most powerful argument.

Socialists, in short, have not shrunk from cosmology, but they have on the whole rejected the monotheistic faiths of Western civilization. In particular socialism rejects the belief that the kingdom of G–d awaits beyond. Ernest Bax, one of the fathers of British Marxism, spoke of "a higher social life in this world . . . whose ultimate possibilities are beyond the power of language to express or thought to conceive."[20] It is in this "that the socialist finds his ideal, his religion." Socialists from Babeuf on have promised a new age of effortless abundance. No one would have to work beyond the age of 25, promised Owen. Man will be free "to hunt in the morning, fish in the afternoon . . . criticize after dinner," said Marx.[21] Once socialism comes, said the famous American socialist author Michael Harrington, "[t]he sentence decreed in the Garden of Eden will have been served."[22]

Harrington points us toward the deeper levels of socialism's appeal when he tells us that "socialism . . . is the idea of an utterly new society in which some of the fundamental limitations of human existence have been transcended."[23] Material want is not the only limit that will be transcended, as Fourier's promise of a sexual minimum reminds us. Indeed, many of the great figures of socialist history exemplified disdain for limits in their own lives. Mao kept a vast harem, Mussolini was a famous womanizer, even the austere Lenin kept a mistress, and Marx impregnated the maid, whose name, by the way was DeMuth (and we at AEI are doing our part to avenge the family's honor.)

I mention these peccadillos not just to keep tune with the times but because I believe they point us to the ultimate element of socialism's appeal. Not only did it perform the happy alchemy of shifting the kingdom of G–d from the next world to this, but it made getting there so much less burdensome. Monotheism had linked cosmology—the understanding of which is a universal human craving—to an ethical system. The establishment of that linkage constituted the single most important step in the progress of mankind. Socialism severed that link. Socialism denied that the path to the kingdom of heaven lay in individual righteousness. Rather it was to be found in political outcomes. The individual could reach it not by striving for moral goodness but by planting himself on the right side of history or of the barricades. Robert Owen explained that what drove him to detest religion was "the . . . absurd [idea] that each [person] . . . determined his own thoughts, will, and action, and was responsible for them to God and his fellow man."[24] This assault on the bonds of individual moral accountability together with the offer of earthly transcendence is what made socialism so sublimely seductive and so terribly destructive.

Is the story of socialism over? I believe it is. Never mind that most of the European Union countries are now under social democratic parties. Whatever those parties offered the voters, it was not socialism. Tony Blair said in his campaign that "Labour is the party of business."[25] The main argument about economics has been settled. But if I am right in believing that the deeper appeal of socialism lay elsewhere, then we can expect that the quest to reach the kingdom of heaven in the here and now, and without having to pay the price of moral rectitude, will reappear in new form, presenting us with tragedies and challenges in the twenty-first century.

Notes

[1]Reprinted in Leo Gershoy, *The Era of the French Revolution 1789–1799: Ten Years that Shook the World* (Princeton: Van Nostrand, 1957) p. 178.

[2]Quoted in R. B. Rose, "Babeuf, Dictatorship and Democracy," *Historical Studies* 15(58): 234.

[3]"November 12, 1825. William H. Shephard to R. H.[L.] Baker," in *Harmony on the Wabash in Transition: from Rapp to Owen*, Karl J. R. Arndt, ed. (Worcester: Harmony Society, 1982), p. 706.

[4]Charles Fourier, *The Amorous World*, quoted in Keith Taylor, *The Political Ideas of the Utopian Socialists* (London: Frank Cass, 1982), p. 121.

[5]Karl Marx and Friedrich Engels, *The Communist Manifesto*, chap. III, sec. 2.

[6]E. J. Hobsbawm, *The Age of Revolution: 1789–1848* (New York: Mentor, 1964), p. 289.

[7]Leszek Kolakowski, "The Golden Age," in *Main Currents of Marxism*, vol. II, P. S. Falla, trans. (Oxford: Clarendon, 1978), p. 1.

[8]Eduard Bernstein, *Evolutionary Socialism* (New York: Schocken, 1961), p. xxii.

[9]V. I. Lenin, *What is to be Done?*, conclusion.

[10]Bernstein, *Evolutionary Socialism*, p. xxix.

[11]Quoted in "China: Deng Xiaoping Leads a Far-Reaching, Audacious but Risky Second Revolution," *Time* (January 6, 1986): 24.

[12]John Darnton, "Labor Won't Try to Undo Thatcherism, Chief Says," *New York Times* (April 3, 1996): 9.

[13]*Le Monde* (October 9, 1982): 14. Translated in FBIS, VII (October 1982): K6.

[14]Quoted in "Africa Makes a Hard Choice," *U.S. News and World Report* (June 27, 1988): 50.

[15]Philippe Buonarroti, *Babeuf's Conspiracy for Equality*, Bronterre O'Brien, trans. (London: H. Hetherington, 1836), p. 230.

[16]Edward Bellamy, *Looking Backward* (New York: Viking Penguin, 1982), p. 105.

[17]Ibid., p. 111.

[18]Aristotle, *The Politics*, book II, chap. 3.

[19]Owen autobiography in *Selected Works of Robert Owen*, vol 4, Gregory Claeys, ed. (London: William Pickering, 1993), p. 155.

[20]Ernest Belfort Bax, *The Religion of Socialism* (Freeport, NY: Books for Libraries Press, 1972), p. 53.

[21]Karl Marx, *The German Ideology*, part IA1.

[22]Michael Harrington, *Socialism* (New York: Bantam, 1973), p. 452.

[23]Ibid., p. 421.

[24]Owen autobiography in *Selected Works*, vol. 4, p. 67.

[25]Fred Barbash, "Tories Face End of an Era," *Washington Post* (May 1, 1997): A1.

CHARLES L. GRISWOLD, JR.

Adam Smith on Distributive Justice, Wealth, and Poverty

> No society can surely be flourishing and happy, of which the far greater part of the members are poor and miserable. It is but equity, besides, that they who feed, cloath and lodge the whole body of the people, should have such a share of the produce of their own labour as to be themselves tolerably well fed, cloathed and lodged.
>
> —Adam Smith, *The Wealth of Nations*[1]

We live in a time that from a historical perspective is extraordinary. Never in history have so many enjoyed so high a level of material prosperity, political and economic liberty, and peace and security. The benefits of the flourishing arts, sciences, and humanistic disciplines are within reach of an unprecedented number of people. We may praise the strict virtues of ancient Sparta, or the high artistic and philosophical accomplishments of ancient Athens, but who among us would willingly return to either, or to any of the great medieval cities, let alone to a less distinguished polis? We are the children of the Enlightenment and scarcely any of us would gladly claim a different patrimony.

And yet scarcely any of us still defend our patrimony without heavy qualifications. Criticism of the modern age and the Enlightenment from which it stems is a staple of our intellectual and spiritual lives, within academia and outside it. The "crisis" literature of the last century and a half remains a prominent part of contemporary rhetoric especially among those who would seem to have least need for it. We do find ourselves faced with unsettling questions, some especially characteristic of our period, and others *quaestiones perennes* that now press with particular force. Some are both. I have just used the pronoun "we"; it is a common locution in philosophy, especially in ethics, as it is in politics. But the question might immediately be put to my use of the word, whether parochialism does not lurk just beneath the surface. True, "we" enjoy a high level of material prosperity, of liberty, and other treasured goods, but how many of our brethren toil in misery just outside the palace door? Is there a sense in which their misery is necessarily the price of our happiness? Is the vast disparity in wealth between rich and poor fair?

It is Adam Smith's legacy, in part, that we now enjoy as well as question. Smith's literary fate is itself a striking case of unexpected inversions and outcomes. Fabled in his own time for his two massively influential books—*The Theory of Moral Sentiments* and *The Wealth of Nations*, Smith's oeuvre gradually became reduced to a single thought lifted from one or two passages of the latter book. The thought was that unfettered capitalism is both just and necessarily productive of wealth. The system of greed and acquisition that ostensibly fuels modern economies is, according to this monumentally distorted picture of Smith, a good thing. As to the gross inequalities of wealth the system generates—these are somehow the just and wise contrivances of nature. These unfortunate readings of Smith are now dead among scholars of the period. In the place of these misreadings, he is being restored to the philosophical canon, and his relevance to the great debates about the modern age is coming back into focus. Smith was a powerful advocate as well as critic of the Enlightenment, as even a superficial reading of his work shows; for that reason alone, it is well worth our study.

My purpose here cannot of course be to assess his thought as a whole. I would like instead to focus on his theory of justice, or rather, on certain aspects of that theory. Justice is a constant thread through Smith's work, showing up as it does in both his books as well as, of course, in his lectures on jurisprudence (of which we have student notes). It is closely connected with his qualified and measured defense of the free market in the *Wealth of Nations*. (I avoid from here on out the term "capitalism" because it is misleading and anachronistic.) And the debates about the justice of the free market, as well as its effectiveness in increasing the "wealth of nations," is perhaps our most immediate point of contact with Smith.

By way of orientation, it is useful to remind ourselves what Smith's intended corpus would have looked like. Smith did not finish his system, but he did intend to present us with a system. Importantly, for present purposes, he finished neither the section treating the principles of natural jurisprudence *simpliciter*, nor the section detailing the way in which the rules of natural jurisprudence evolved over time. We have two sets of student lecture notes that certainly describe this much more "historical" second project; but of course student notes are not entirely reliable.[2]

A second point about this projected corpus: Political economy is a branch of moral philosophy. This is easily missed, not only because of our contemporary habit of separating the two, but because Smith otherwise does not, in one published book, cite himself, or refer, or even—with certain exceptions—allude to his other published book.[3] T*he Wealth of Nations* is not a value-free work in "economics'" in the contemporary sense. It is, rather, framed by moral concepts, that of justice being one. The theory of "natural jurisprudence" Smith hoped to work out was a normative and not merely descriptive theory ("natural" in this context being contrasted with "conventional").

Let us note, third, that the theory of moral sentiments proposes to treat two questions: "What is virtue," and (in his own words) "By what power or faculty in the mind is it, that this character, whatever it be, is recommended to us? Or in other words, how and by what means does it come to pass, that the mind prefers one tenour of conduct to another, denominates the one right and the other wrong; considers the one as the object of approbation, honour, and reward, and the other of blame, censure, and punishment?" (VII.i.2). This second question is what I shall call the "moral psychology" question.

Smith's theory of justice is founded in his moral psychology—in particular, his view of the passions, of sympathy, of the impartial spectator, and of propriety. I cannot adequately cover so much ground in this essay. So I shall say something briefly about the notion of propriety, the passion of resentment, and several other assumptions that contribute to Smith's doctrine of moral individualism. This will provide us sufficient basis for a transition to the theory of justice, liberty, and property as expressed in *The Wealth of Nations*.

In discussing the contributions made by his predecessors to the two questions analyzed by a theory of moral sentiments, Smith sets out the following alternatives:

VIRTUE	MORAL PSYCHOLOGY
as propriety (the ancients, Smith)	self-love (Hobbes, Mandeville)
as prudence (Epicurus)	reason (Cudworth)
as benevolence (Hutcheson)	sentiments
	(a) moral sense (Hutcheson)
	(b.i) based on utility (Hume)
	(b.ii) based on sympathy (Smith)

Smith takes himself as a propriety theorist with respect to the virtue question, and a sentiments theorist with respect to the moral psychology question. Roughly speaking, Smith sees himself as synthesizing an ancient view about the nature of virtue with a modern doctrine (whose development owes much to him) about the sources of moral approval.

Smith's answer to the question "what is virtue" is that it consists in the "proper government and direction of all our affections," and not in that of any one type of sentiment (whether the selfish or other-regarding). "Virtue consists in propriety" (VII.ii.intro.1); that is, it consists in the appropriate "pitch" of the given passion (VII.ii.1.12; cf. *Nichomachean Ethics* 1106b36–1107a2). Smith explains at length that the "mean" will differ depending on the type of passion at issue (I.ii.intro.2; VI.iii.14-18). Aristotle tells us that the mean is relative "to us" (*pros hemas; Nichomachean Ethics* 1107a1), and in a sense Smith agrees. *Orthos logos* (right reason) is determined by the impartial spectator (this is Smith's version of Aristotle's "ideal judge" theory, the theory of the *phronimos* as the measure). In other words, that which is "right" and "good" will be defined relative to the responses and judgments of a person whose dispositions and knowledge of the situation are of an appropriate sort.

Smith distinguishes between two "aspects" under which motive, action, or character may be considered, although in common life we "constantly" evaluate under both these aspects. The first "aspect" is "propriety." Propriety and its contrary lie in the "suitableness or un- suitableness, in the proportion or disproportion which the affection seems to bear to the cause or object which excites it." (I.i.3.6). The second "aspect" concerns merit or demerit, which lie in "the beneficial or hurtful nature of the effects which the affection aims at, or tends to produce," that is, "the qualities by which it is entitled to reward, or is deserving of punishment" (I.i.3.7). Roughly speaking, then, our judg- ments of virtue and vice normally evaluate the reasonableness of a sen- timent or action (a) relative to the cause or object that prompts it, and (b) relative to the consequences engendered by the agent.

Since in *The Theory of Moral Sentiments,* Part VII, Smith defines virtue altogether as "propriety," it seems strange that propriety is cast early on in the book as only one of the "aspects" in question. But in fact the second "aspect" (merit) is also built up from considerations of "propriety.[4] The sense of merit is "a compounded sentiment, and to be made up of two distinct emotions; a direct sympathy with the sentiments of the agent, and an indirect sympathy with the gratitude of those who receive the benefit of his actions" (II.1.4.2; so too with the sense of demerit). Smith comes close to saying that "direct sym- pathy" comes to a judgment of the propriety of the actor's motive, and our "indirect sympathy" to an evaluation of the appropriateness of the recipient's joy or distress. When we think the motives of the agent to be mean, for example, we are not disposed to enter into the gratitude of the recipient, since the agent seems not to deserve grat- itude. When we approve the agent's motives, we do not sympathize with the recipient's distress (II.1.3.1).

Unless we be perfectly virtuous, general moral rules will form part of our moral consciousness, as will a conversation that brings them and the case at hand together. It may seem strange that a moral philosopher who places so much emphasis on virtue, as Smith does, also has a theory of the importance of moral rules. How does Smith understand these rules?

Very briefly: He distinguishes between two kinds of moral rules. One kind resembles the rules of grammar; these rules are precise, and determine with exactitude our obligations. The rules of justice are of this sort. Without "tolerable observance" of the rules of justice, human society "would crumble into nothing" (III.5.2; III.3.6). The importance of "grammatical" rules is in proportion to their role in the avoidance of conflict and war. Important as they are, the place in the moral universe for rules of this sort is strictly limited. The profoundly misguided attempt to create similar "rules for the conduct of a good man" is at the heart of casuistry (VII.iv.8; cf. VII.iv.34). In fact "it belongs to feeling and sentiment only to judge" of moral virtues other than justice (VII.iv.33).

This said, we need to go further: What sentiments in particular are at play here? And specifically what sense of "justice" does Smith have in mind?

The word "justice" has several, historically shifting senses. This makes confusion about the topic easy right from the start. In the course of his discussion of Plato in Part VII of *The Theory of Moral Sentiments*, Smith helpfully distinguishes between several meanings of the term (VII.ii.1.10). The first sense amounts to "commutative" justice, and concerns specifications of and punishments for harm one might do to another's person, property, or reputation. This is the sense Smith analyzes in this book, and in characterizing a person as "just" we too seem to have this sense in mind.

He claims that his notion coincides with what Aristotle meant by commutative justice (VII.ii.1.10), but that is not quite accurate, for the corresponding part of justice in Aristotle's scheme is the *diorthotikon dikaion* (*Nichomachean Ethics* 1131a1 and context), that is, corrective justice, which rectifies inequalities in voluntary or involuntary exchanges between individuals. Smith's "commutative" justice seems a bit broader than Aristotle's, since it specifies wrongs and punishments in any area in which force may be used to compel obedience, and this may include groups as well as individuals. Thus businesses that have monopolies that in turn preclude other individuals or groups from entering the market may be commutatively unjust. A sovereign who is not impartial between nonfanatical religions, or who does not administer justice in a regular and impartial way, or who does not obey the law, is commutatively unjust. Smith includes in commutative justice a notion of "fair play."

Smith also specifies a second, broader sense of justice. According to it, we do justice to someone when we positively "exert ourselves to serve him and to place him in that situation in which the impartial spectator would be pleased to see him." Smith thinks this is what some thinkers, such as Grotius, call distributive justice. It need not be discharged by the sovereign or state. Smith understands this "distributive justice" as "proper beneficence," as the exercise of charity, generosity, liberality, and other social virtues, and this more or less folds it into his discussion of beneficence in *The Theory of Moral Sentiments,* Part VI. This sense of "justice" covers what can be morally required of people in their dealings with others.[5]

We tend somewhat vaguely to think of distributive justice as a duty the state or sovereign is alone charged with, one that goes beyond commutative justice because it entails the allotment of such things as rights, opportunities, advantages, offices, entitlements, duties, taxes, even risks, in accordance with need or desert. This may include the forcible redistribution of goods held in private insofar as they, like these other items, are in some way the result of society's cooperative endeavor. Often the goal is to rectify an inequality or unfavorable condition some person or group experiences due to no fault of its own, but traceable somehow to the basic structure of the society's institutions or communal traditions and practices. When we think about market societies, the problems of distribution and inequality strike us as particularly pressing. We have in mind issues of the fair distribution of wealth and opportunities, as well as issues of equality of opportunity and a decent standard of life, of disparities in class and power, and indeed of the role of fortune or luck in determining people's chances to better their condition. These issues struck Smith too as pressing both morally and prudentially, and *The Wealth of Nations* is full of comments about justice and inequality. Yet for reasons I will discuss in a moment, he recommends commutative justice as the controlling model.[6]

Justice differs from the other virtues in a number of ways. It seems preeminently a social or political virtue, bearing on the relations required for the very existence of community in a way that other virtues do not. The principles or rules which define justice are ordinarily taken as enforceable in a way that, say, the rules of benevolence are not. The rules specifying what actions justice requires or prohibits are more precise than those of the other virtues; as we have seen, Smith compares them to the rules of grammar. Further, justice is distinct in that it is a primarily "negative virtue" (II.ii.1.9), defined in terms of abstention from wrongdoing. While Smith insists on the distinctness of justice in these ways, he also holds that justice is a virtue or excellence of character, though not quite in the same way that other virtues are admirable dispositions of self.

Smith's effort to combine a virtue ethics inspired by the ancients with a doctrine of virtue that supports a modern jurisprudential framework of commutative justice and rights is as intriguing as it is controversial.[7] Virtues as well as rights, excellencies of character as well as "juridical" moral rules, have their roots in his moral psychology, and he views them as indispensable to a flourishing liberal commercial polity. As we will discuss in a moment, the sense of justice, and therewith the whole jurisprudential structure built on it, is itself founded in a sense of resentment such as would be approved by an impartial spectator. Because Smith largely leaves distributive justice up to private benevolence, the proper sense of compassion, and thus the education of imagination and "sympathy" are crucial. The restriction of justice to the commutative makes benevolence more, not less, important.[8]

The topic of justice first arises in *The Theory of Moral Sentiments* in the course of Smith's analysis of merit (and so that which is deserving of reward) and demerit (and so that which is deserving of punishment). These are types of approbation or disapprobation of motives and actions distinct from judgments of propriety and impropriety, and are tied (as already remarked) to the "beneficial or hurtful effects which the affection proposes or tends to produce." That is, merit and demerit consist in good or ill desert, the moral praise and blame of which will be prompted by certain emotions; in this case, gratitude and resentment, mediated by sympathy with the persons acting and acted upon, as felt from the perspective of the "reasonable man" (II.i.2.3).[9] These passions belong to those derived from the imagination (I.ii.2.1). Thus Smith's theory of justice grows organically out of the psychology of sympathetic imagination.

Resentment is "never properly called forth but by actions which tend to do real and positive hurt to some particular persons" (II.ii.1.4).

Each part of this statement is important to Smith's account, for it serves as the basis for drawing a crucial distinction between justice and beneficence, and for narrowing the relevant sense of justice to the commutative. Let us focus on the criterion of "real and positive hurt." How is that to be understood?

The notion of "illusive sympathy" is crucial here, for as spectators we are called upon, in the case where the greatest harm has been done to another—the taking of his or her life—to place ourselves in the position of the deceased and to imagine the anger and resentment that person would feel. The harm which "in our fancy" the deceased has undergone calls forth, under the right conditions, "sympathetic tears" and "sympathetic indignation" and hence our powerful desire to punish the perpetrator (II.i.2.5; II.i.5.6). This is simply an extension of Smith's discussion, at the end of the very first chapter of *The Theory of Moral Sentiments*, of our sympathy with the dead which depends on an "illusion of the imagination," thanks to which we put "our own living souls in their inanimated bodies, and thence conceiving what would be our emotions in this case." This is the illusion which leads us to dread death, an illusion that is "the great restraint upon the injustice of mankind" (I.i.1.13). In other words, the sense of commutative justice is an extension of the imagination's prephilosophical self-regulation, so to speak, thanks to which we may govern ourselves and live in tolerable harmony.

What then is the basic hierarchy of harms? Since "death is the greatest evil which one man can inflict upon another" and thus "excites the highest degree of resentment," murder is the greatest of crimes against an individual. There next follows harm to one's person, first one's body, then extensions of self such as one's reputation. Then comes property, the deprivation of which is a greater harm than disappointment of an expectation, then (II.ii.2.2).[10] This hierarchy of wrongs reflects levels of resentment felt by the impartial spectator, whose role Smith is here assuming. Because we (the pronoun is very common in these pages) feel this emotion in these respects, we are moved to punish the doer of harm as well as forcibly to compel adherence to precise rules that prohibit the harm. The rules aimed at preventing the unwarranted causing of pain have this peculiar urgency, and are taken to be compulsory. These rules are the principles of justice.

By contrast, failure of an agent to exercise proper benevolence does "no real positive evil." It may disappoint, hurt, anger, and even lead to condemnation of the agent; but it does not warrant resentment and hence the use of punitive force. Therefore beneficence may not be legally compelled nor its absence punished by force. We are under obligations of "perfect and complete obligation" to perform the duties of justice, but not of any of the other virtues. Beneficence is "always free" in this jurisprudential sense, while justice is not "left to the freedom of our own wills" (II.ii.1.5). In according pain this peculiar salience, Smith is articulating as a fact of moral psychology an ethical view about what is and what is not endurable by a person of good character.[11]

Having laid the foundations in his discussion of (de)merit, the passions of gratitude and resentment and their connection with reward and punishment, and in the difference between hurt feelings and "real positive evil," Smith is prepared to define "justice" as the obligatory regard for principles of conduct whose violation causes, in the judgment of an impartial spectator, real harm and arouses warranted resentment as well as a demand for proportionate punishment (II.ii.1.4, 5). Justice and retaliation are inseparable (II.ii.1.10). Smith has thus explained several of the differences between commutative justice and the other virtues—the sense of obligation that accompanies it, its "negative" character, and its particular connection with harm and pain. Not just the urgency, but the exactitude of the rules governing justice seem connected with the fact that the marked "pungency" or sharpness of pain (I.iii.1.3) allows us to detect differences between kinds and amounts of pain with relative precision.[12] The close connection between commutative justice, specific actions, and external goods such as property, brings it into a public and visible arena that facilitates estimation by spectators of just how much wrong has been done, how much the agent should be punished, and how much must be restored to the sufferer in order to balance the scales. By contrast, if I have failed to show you the proper degree of friendship, how is a spectator to discern with any distinctness how much justified harm has been caused, and what punishment the state ought inflict? Expert discernment in such matters is better left to finely sensitive novelists, rather than to jurists whose decisions are enforced by police powers.[13]

Since the impartial spectator's resentment will be aroused by specific actions directed at specific individuals causing specific injury, judgments about the agent's injustice will not in the first instance be judgments about the agent's character, life plan, scheme of virtues, or happiness. Hence Smith's use of the term "fair play" here; the agent may "in the race for wealth, and honours, and preferments," run "as hard as he can, and strain every nerve and every muscle, in order to outstrip all his competitors," and the spectators may well think the entire competition to be silly and driven by some "deception" of the imagination. But impartial spectators will not *resent* the agent's playing (or winning) of the game unless he "should justle, or throw down any of them [his competitors]," for that violates "fair play." In the spectator's judgment about *merit*, the "right" and the "good" are distinct. The spectator has no reason to grant the agent's partiality or selfish bias in favor of himself (II.ii.2.1). This "fair play" conception of justice requires neither equality of outcome in the game, nor equality of starting points (e.g., in skills at playing the game), as Smith's qualified reconciliation with the fact of a social hierarchy of wealth and power indicates.

Being commutatively just "does no real positive good" and may sometimes be fulfilled by "sitting still and doing nothing" (II.ii.1.9). The just person may therefore seem to be a sort of moral blank slate, a rights bearer devoid of virtue. One might infer that the virtue consists simply in obeying rules, and as these define what one ought not to do, that justice is only a quasi-virtue. On that interpretation there would seem to be no connection between commutative justice that is understood as a political phenomenon and justice as a disposition of self, that is, as a virtue of character. Consequently there may seem to be little connection between political justice and any of the other virtues.[14] The problem here is one very much at the heart of contemporary discussions about the relationship between civic and individual virtue, especially in the context of a liberal society.

The divorce between political justice and just character cannot be complete, for the just person is not *simply* someone who consistently follows rules prohibiting harm to others. Rather, he or she is governed by a reverence for rules of justice, and a determined resolve never to be guilty of positively hurting others. Smith's language in this regard is striking. He speaks over and over again of the just person's "conscientious," "sacred," and "religious" respect for the "sacred" rules of justice.[15] Even when sitting still and causing no harm throughout his life, the just person demonstrates a "habitual reverence" for the principles of justice. This constitutes a "positive" character trait. The existence of society not only depends on a tolerable observation of these basic principles (III.3.6, III.5.2), it "cannot subsist among those who are at all times ready to hurt and injure one another" (II.ii.3.3). The just person not only abstains from hurting others, he is not ever *ready* to hurt others without warrant, and this is a fixed disposition of character.

Smith's remarkable language about the just person's "religious" regard for the rules of justice is complemented by an equally remarkable passage in which he discusses the unfortunate case in which a just person has unintentionally harmed an innocent. Just as the holy ground consecrated to a god in a pagan religion is never to be trespassed upon, so "the happiness of every innocent man is, in the same manner, rendered holy, consecrated, and hedged round against the approach of every other man; not to be wantonly trod upon, not even to be, in any respect, ignorantly and involuntarily violated, without requiring some expiation, some atonement in proportion to the greatness of such undesigned violation" (II.iii.3.4). The rules of justice are "sacred" because what they protect—the human individual—is as sacred as is the domain of a god. This ringing declaration of the sanctity of the individual is at the heart of Smith's moral philosophy and political economy; it is the moral basis of the famous "system of natural liberty" advocated by *The Wealth of Nations*.[16] Thus the concern requisite for warranted resentment is not prompted by thought of the welfare of society so much as by "the general fellow-feeling which we have with every man merely because he is our fellow-creature" (II.ii.3.10). That respect will be part of the character of the just person. So deeply rooted in most of us is this respect, that even a person whose character is corrupt will likely feel, after the fact, its effects.[17]

Smith is working, in sum, with the intuitive idea that justice is fundamentally tied to our (the spectator's or bystander's) resentment at the infliction of what we judge to be unwarranted pain or harm (that is, injury). The "negative" character of justice stems from this original association, as does the idea that to do justice is to balance the scales, to reciprocate by making up what was lost through takings from the perpetrator. Smith resists revising these basic intuitions, and instead explains their basis (the theory of sympathy, pleasure and pain, and the passions) as well as the jurisprudence that would follow (a jurisprudence of rights, as specified by impartial spectators in the given historical context). It is a normative jurisprudence that stays for the most part within the conceptual bounds of commutative justice, and bases itself on a doctrine of individual liberty and of moral equality among individuals. His view is part of his egalitarian outlook, which may also be termed "moral individualism." Given the importance of "sympathy" to Smith's account, we may also say that Smith is promoting a system of "sympathetic liberalism."[18]

In setting out his hierarchy of wrongs, Smith implicitly asks us to agree that piety and justice are different from each other in such a way that we do not resent accusations about the falsity or perverseness of an agent's religious views as much as we would other harms. This may well be the enlightened view of the matter. Yet one could easily imagine a setting in which the mere presence of a religious view incompatible with one's own—let alone a loudly established presence—would cause a person profound pain and provoke indignant resentment. One might very well be moved to punish the "infidels" harshly on the grounds that they are persuaded of views repulsive to any civilized person. Just as we no longer hesitate to trod on a precinct once sacred to a heathen god—to recall again Smith's own analogy—so we might not hesitate to stamp down the infidels who dwell in any such precinct, precisely because of our resentment at the harm we feel their presence causes. Smith objects that such things as religious differences and the failure of others to sympathize with and endorse one's own faith may hurt; but that they do not cause the kind of harm that in an impartial spectator would provoke resentment and the desire to punish. To deny this is to start down the path to twisted resentments, "fanaticism," and eventually the "inquisition."

Smith's reply may be charged with begging the question. Has he not simply *assumed* a view of the natural or healthy functioning of the moral sentiments, and so of resentment, without offering any argument to the effect that construing "harm" in the manner of the "fanatic" is corrupt? This is finally a question about the thrust of both the virtue theory and the moral psychology. Enlightenment "arguments" against religion often seem, on inspection, to be more polemical denunciations than careful philosophical refutations; is Smith's theory of justice a covert instance of this tendency?

Smith does have resources at his command for replying to this charge of begging the question. First, he may draw on the same resources available to him in other disputes (such as arguments about slavery or infanticide). These include the demand that we pay close, sympathetic attention to the contested phenomena (Smith is fond of literary tragedies that insightfully and movingly explore the ethical and psychological consequences of religious zeal). The effort will be, in part, to show how supposed purity of religious motivation inflicts unacceptable harm, and masks vanity or some other blameworthy passion. Second, Smith has at his disposal an argument about the deleterious social and political effects of state-supported religion.[19] Part of the argument is that in various ways religion undermines its own claims when it uses the police powers of the state to institute its dogma. If true, this is a compelling critique.

Third, Smith can reply that his view about what constitutes "real positive evil" is not viciously circular, because the moral psychology is not fitted to one and only one set of virtues. He also deploys it when discussing the quite different conceptions of virtues of Native Americans, residents of distant centuries and places, and so forth. The theory of "natural jurisprudence," which is based on the impartial spectator theory, is supple enough to explain many different historical schemes of justice.[20]

But if one wants a "proof" generated from outside any broad ethical scheme, then one wants something Smith cannot provide. Moral criticism must take a more piecemeal approach, and in the present instance this would include a dialectical response: Why, he would ask, is a proof that stands outside any ethical frame required? What would such a proof look like? Since you are demanding a demonstration of this sort from me, can you provide one supporting *your* view of the matter? The conversation would unfold from there.

Smith's decision to focus on commutative or rectificatory justice, and for the most part to assimilate distributive justice to benevolence, does not proceed out of indifference to the lot of the less fortunate, or from blindness to any claims of equity. He is committed to the view that humanity ought to enjoy a decent standard of living. Smith's spirited defense of commutative justice in *The Wealth of Nations*, his outrage against legal and political arrangements that deny people their liberty to dispose of their labor as they think best, and his obvious commitment to a political economy that will benefit the poor, testify to his moral outlook.[21] Yet in spite of the statement quoted at the start of this essay, he does not advocate—on grounds that its recipients are owed a decent standard of living, equality of opportunity, or equity—anything like an ongoing scheme for state redistribution of goods.

The explanation is multilayered. To begin with, as already noted, Smith is assuming that principles of justice must be capable of precise specification. They cannot resemble, as we have seen, the rules specifying the duties of friendship, for these are "loose, vague, and indeterminate," and it is extremely difficult to say with precision what would constitute their violation. As the state will bring its enormous police powers to bear in enforcing rules of justice, it is crucial that these rules be specifiable, explicable, and knowable with precision. I take Smith to be holding that beyond the rules of commutative justice, we cannot meet these criteria. Smith repeatedly insists on "the exact administration of justice" (*The Wealth of Nations*, IV.ix.51; V.i.b.1; V.i.c.2); this duty is one of three he ascribes to the sovereign. Distributive justice is not a promising candidate for exact administration.

Determining equity would hinge in part on specifying who is to take responsibility (and to what degree) for the situation to be redressed. Determining what is beyond a person's control is, of course, an extremely controversial matter. Especially given the role of luck in human life, it would be very hard to sort out the mix of fortune, individual responsibility, and social responsibility that constitute a person's opportunities. Smith himself emphasizes the formative role which the family, properly structured (e.g., so as to exclude polygamy), plays in the moral education of the individual. As different families will discharge their responsibilities differently, the opportunities of individuals are bound to vary. What is the individual owed in compensation for any deficiencies in upbringing? Outside the sphere of commutative justice, Smith largely suspends judgment about that mix, so far as state intervention is concerned. In general, individuals cannot be indemnified by the state against bad consequences arising from factors outside their control.

Smith is not denying that harm can be done in a way that, ideally, would warrant redress beyond what commutative justice can offer. He understands, as his historical accounts of the genesis of various schemes of justice indicate, that even if the playing field is level, the players come to it with varying degrees of skill and advantage.[22] He begins *The Wealth of Nations* by denying that differences in ability— for example, between a porter and a philosopher—are natural, ascribing them primarily to the effects of the division of labor, education, and the like. He advocates removal of any commutatively unjust measures that preclude the porter from becoming a philosopher, or vice versa, and asserts that such must be done with humanity (*The Wealth of Nations* IV.ii.40). But he thinks there no equitable way, on the whole, to specify within a jurisprudential framework how goods are to be (re)distributed so as to remove the inequalities in the "opportunities" of individual players. This is *a fortiori* so in a complex commercial society, for there the relationship between an individual and his or her opportunities, as well as between the individual and social or political arrangements, is bound to be enormously tangled.

Smith frequently emphasizes that the legislator lacks sufficient knowledge to direct individuals in their decisions about employing labor. It is not only unjust of the state to control the individual's distribution of his efforts, it is folly for good epistemic reasons as well. Generally speaking, individuals are far better positioned to assess their own actual and potential abilities, risks, and the particulars of local opportunities. This point is made in both *The Theory of Moral Sentiments* (VI.ii.1.1) and *The Wealth of Nations*.[23] This point would apply to the state's effort to redistribute goods to the deserving; assessing in a consistent way who the deserving are, and just what they are due, lies beyond the ken of the legislator or statesman.

Smith is generally skeptical of the abilities as well as the motivations of the legislator or statesman, excepting the most philosophical of these, and he does not expect the philosophers to rule (*The Wealth of Nations* V.i.f.51). Ever the clearheaded realist, he fully expects those with power to lean toward their own self-interest even when they assume the mantle of public benefactor.[24] As he puts it, the authority needed to direct the affairs of private individuals could not "safely be trusted" to any single person or council or senate "whatever," let alone to someone presumptuous enough to think he could exercise the authority wisely (*The Wealth of Nations* IV.ii.9). He doubts there exists a "remedy" for the "violence and injustice of the rulers of mankind."[25] He speaks of a "legislator" who is "guided by general principles which are always the same"—and who thus sounds rather like a Platonic philosopher-king—but contrasts him with "that insidious and crafty animal, vulgarly called a statesman or politician"; it is clear that the latter run the world (*The Wealth of Nations* IV.ii.39). His comments about the partiality of merchants and businesspeople toward their own interests could not be more condemnatory; indeed he views them as almost always engaging in a "conspiracy against the publick" (e.g., *The Wealth of Nations* I.x.c.27; IV.iii.c.10). The legislature seems dominated by the "clamorous importunity of partial interests" (*The Wealth of Nations* IV.ii.44), and for Smith this is typical of the public sphere.

When states are charged with the delicate task of redistributing wealth so as to correct inequities, and of equalizing not just the playing field but the ability of the players to compete on an equal footing, there are grave dangers of abuse of power requisite to so large a task, including those of self-promotion and self-perpetuation by the self-interested and unwise class of politicians. A scheme for distributive justice risks becoming what we would call an unfunded mandate, or at least a mandate whose extent and duration seems impossible to specify in advance. Smith's skeptical comments about the conceits of the "man of system" (e.g., VI.ii.2.15–17) mesh well with *The Wealth of Nations*' stance here.[26] Incorrectly handled, distributive justice risks generating resentment, indeed warranted resentment, and therefore both social instability and the devolution of "sympathy" into selfishness. It risks transforming the state from an impartial umpire into a selectively benevolent parent. And as always unforeseen and negative consequences may be generated by the noblest of impulses.

I have hedged my formulations of this issue, for Smith does propose some schemes for equity, that for compulsory education being one of the most important.[27] While in typically nondogmatic fashion Smith leaves room for measures such as these, he nonetheless makes clear that they are provoked by the grossest deformities in the condition of the poor, deformities so great as to threaten the survival of the nation. While the motivation from grounds of humanity is clear, he does not actually say the poor are *owed* this publicly funded education as a matter of justice, but that public utility demands they be subjected to it—so long of course as the means chosen are very carefully thought through so as to prevent the evils that always accompany the creation of state-enforced standards (e.g., the creation of administrators of those standards, in this case teachers, whose income is assured). When discussing the question as to whether the government ought redistribute food in case of a famine, for example, by ordering corn dealers to sell their food stock at what the government considers to be a reasonable price, Smith objects on grounds of both efficiency and justice. The "unlimited, unrestrained freedom of the corn trade" is in fact the best preventative against famines, and corn traders also deserve to charge more during times of dearth in order to recoup profits they lost during normal times (*The Wealth of Nations* IV.v.b.7, 8).[28]

Smith has to a large extent shifted the problem of caring for the "laboring poor" to the market, and has dropped to that extent the traditional problem as to the moral bearing that the genesis of inequality (e.g., the problem of the "original" division of the land) should have on the redistribution of goods. He takes it for granted that all sorts of inequalities, many unjustified according to the standards of commutative justice, have developed over time. Let me point out that to advocate that the market, under conditions of liberty and commutative justice, be largely entrusted with alleviating these inequalities, and so the condition of the poor, makes at least two large assumptions of an empirical nature.

The first is that under these conditions, people's resentments at ancient harms will fade and, therewith, demands for rectification. The impartial spectator's imagination is definitive of what constitutes a harm in need of rectification, and the moral imagination is not expected to entertain forever a long chain of harms stretching back through time and across changing circumstances. Second, Smith is arguing that the free market (and so a system of natural liberty and justice) will in fact improve the condition of the poor, and do so much more effectively than mercantilist schemes, for example.[29] Were he mistaken about this distributive result of the operation of the "invisible hand" (*The Theory of Moral Sentiments* IV.i.10), then it would seem fair to say that his stance on the question of distributive justice is jeopardized on its own grounds. This is a case in which economic theory is carrying a significant moral burden.

It is inevitable that in some historical instantiations of the "system of natural liberty," the condition of the laboring poor will *not* be improving. Judging whether or not the *system* is to be rejected altogether is necessarily complex for two reasons. First, as Smith himself points out, any actual liberal and commercial society will only approximate the "Utopia" of a "system of natural liberty" (*The Wealth of Nations* IV.ii.43). Thus it can always be claimed that its failings under present conditions result from its lack of adequate implementation. Second, he presents us in Book III of *The Wealth of Nations* with a theory of the "natural progress of opulence" through gradual stages (those of agriculture, manufacturing, and foreign trade). He is not proposing that a free society can be pumped into any historical context whatever, like a magic vaccine into the body politic, with beneficial results. Thanks to various historical contingencies, it is possible for a society to skip stages in its development by, say, building up its manufacturing capacity before its agriculture is sufficiently productive. But that will introduce various strains, and these indict not so much the system of natural liberty as the way in which it has been grafted onto a particular society at a particular historical juncture. Or so Smith wishes to argue.

One's affirmation of a particular theory of political economy must be informed, we infer, by an appreciation of its virtues relative to the competition, and these must be understood at least in part through historical analysis. Smith's argument in *The Wealth of Nations* is indirectly supported by his argument against alternatives, such as mercantilist and physiocratic views. He would certainly push the defender of classical polities to justify both the system of slavery on which they were built and their general poverty (cf. Smith's comment at *The Wealth of Nations* III.ii.9 on the "city in speech" of Plato's *Laws*). The defense of his own view of the *best practicable* society is, as always in his work, multifaceted, dialectical, a blend of empirical and philosophical reasoning. It is backed up by appeals to justice as well as to wise judgment.

Smith's account invites many questions, among which we may mention the following. First, how enthusiastic an endorsement has Smith really provided of the "system of natural liberty" (of which the free market is one part), given his own comments about the natural rapacity of businesspeople, the corruptibility of governments, and the like?[30] Smith argues that the widespread and ineradicable effort on the part of each of us to "better his condition" normally takes the form of the pursuit of wealth.[31] Yet that pursuit depends on what Smith himself calls a "deception of the imagination" (*The Theory of Moral Sentiments* IV.1.10).

Second, how does he respond to criticisms to the effect that the free market exploits, dehumanizes, or objectifies the worker? Smith's own commentary on the deleterious effects of the free market on the workers is unrivalled in its poignancy and power.[32]

Third, what of the criticisms to the effect that the "system of natural liberty" subverts itself, as though through the intervention of the "invisible hand"? For example, John Gray has argued that the free market destabilizes the political and social conditions needed for its own stable functioning.[33]

By way of conclusion, a few words that obliquely address the last of these questions. Smith understands that politics is the art of the imperfect; in the felicitous phrase of another commentator, he is an advocate of the "politics of imperfection."[34] His emphasis on liberty reflects his conception not just of the moral primacy of the individual, but also of the serious obstructions faced by any notion of a "science" of politics. His political economy and doctrine of justice are formulated against the backdrop of a picture of human finitude and its political and social consequences. The distinction between best and second best standards of perfection is certainly familiar to us from classical political philosophy. We detect here once again, at a comprehensive systematic level, Smith's sensitivity to propriety—to the requirements of harmony, balance, appropriateness, measure.

How is the "system of natural liberty" to be reconciled with the rejection of systematic politics, or the wisdom of the "great legislator" with the insistence on imperfection? The answer is in part that this "system" of liberty is actually the other side of his skepticism about system. It is a system that liberates politics from system, a sort of anti-utopian utopianism. While positive action is required to maintain the system of natural liberty, it generally takes the form of removing obstacles to it and then of responding to the unavoidable and unforeseeable self-underminings as they occur.[35] Under such a "natural" system, the great philosophical legislators would be relieved of the burden of ruling. And this, Smith might argue, would not only fulfill the demands of justice to the bulk of humankind—those whose condition Smith is most interested in ameliorating—but also prevent injustice to philosophers who ought rather to be occupied with exactly the sort of thing you and I are doing at this very moment.[36]

Notes

[1] *The Wealth of Nations* I.viii.36. Marx picks up on his passage (and blends it with others as well as with his own views) when he remarks: "Since, however, according to Smith a society is not happy in which the majority suffers, and since the wealthiest state of society leads to suffering for the majority, while the economic system (in general, a society of private interests) leads to this wealthiest state, it follows that social *misery* is the goal of the economy." First of the "Economic and Philosophical Manuscripts" (1844), in *Karl Marx: Early Writings*, T. B. Bottomore, ed. & trans. (New York: McGraw-Hill, 1964), p. 74. I have used the Glasgow Edition of Smith's texts throughout this paper, as follows: *The Theory of Moral Sentiments*, A. L. Macfie and D. D. Raphael, eds. (Indianapolis: Liberty Press, 1982); *An Inquiry into the Nature and Causes of the Wealth of Nations*, R. H. Campbell and A. S. Skinner, eds., 2 vols. (Indianapolis: Liberty Press, 1976); *Lectures on Jurisprudence*, R. L. Meek and D. D. Raphael, eds. (Indianapolis: Liberty Press, 1982). Unless otherwise noted, paginal references to Smith's text advert to *The Theory of Moral Sentiments*.

[2] This means that setting out Smith's theory of justice is hobbled from the start. At the end of his life, Smith had quite a few manuscripts consigned to the flames, presumably those containing drafts of his thoughts on jurisprudence were included. Why did he not finish this work, or allow it to be published? Speculations range from the absence of time—his own explanation—to the intrinsic incompletability of at least the first mentioned project (articulating the principles of natural jurisprudence *simpliciter*) given other aspects of Smith's theoretical apparatus.

[3] At *Lectures on Jurisprudence*(B)12, Smith refers his students to *The Theory of Moral Sentiments*. In the context of oral lectures, that is, Smith made some

effort to tie together his written work; but what is appropriate in a classroom may not be in a published document. For a detailed explanation of Smith's projected corpus, please see my *Adam Smith and the Virtues of Enlightenment* (Cambridge: Cambridge University Press, 1999), Introduction section 5.

[4]As is argued by Haakonssen, *The Science of a Legislator* (Cambridge: Cambridge University Press, 1981), p. 64. Smith uses the language of "propriety" in defining merit (e.g., II.i.4.1, 2, 4).

[5]*The Theory of Moral Sentiments* VII.ii.1.10. For a discussion of the background of Smith's views on distributive justice in Grotius, Pufendorf, and Locke, see I. Hont and M. Ignatieff's "Needs and Justice in the 'Wealth of Nations,'" in *Wealth and Virtue*, I. Hont and M. Ignatieff, eds. (Cambridge: Cambridge University Press, 1983), part IV. Smith notes that Aristotle's sense of distributive justice is different in that it "consists in the proper distribution of rewards from the public stock of a community," i.e., in the allocation of public goods to specifiable individuals whose merit to them is determinable. Smith does not think distributive justice in Aristotle's sense to be the task of the state, since it would amount to distribution of public goods (or the forced redistribution of private goods) according to the moral virtue of the recipients, i.e., in accordance with moral desert.

[6]Controlling but not exclusive: even in *The Theory of Moral Sentiments*, as when he declares that "the mere justice is, *upon most occasions*, but a negative virtue" (II.ii.1.9; emphasis added), the door is left open for something more "positive."

[7]Cf. J. G. A. Pocock's "Cambridge Paradigms and Scotch Philosophers: a Study of the Relations between the Civic Humanist and the Civil Jurisprudential Interpretation of Eighteenth-Century Social Thought," in *Wealth and Virtue: the Shaping of Political Economy in the Scottish Enlightenment*, I. Hont and M. Ignatieff, eds. (Cambridge: Cambridge University Press, 1985), pp. 249–52. Pocock comments on the prominent but still unsolved problem of reconciling civic humanism and civil jurisprudence, especially in the context of Smith's thought. More than one commentator has found Smith's attempted synthesis impossible, and therefore that Smith's "Aristotelian" virtue-ethics talk is "vestigial" relative to his modern jurisprudential talk. For the "vestige" term and view see J. Cropsey's *Polity and Economy* (Westport, CT: Greenwood Press, 1977), pp. x, 79. See also Minowitz' *Profits, Priests, and Princes* (Stanford: Stanford University Press, 1993), p. 133 (he calls these "danglers" as well); and V. Brown's *Adam Smith's Discourse: Canonicity, Commerce and Conscience* (London: Routledge, 1994), p. 212. On page 94 of *Polity and Economy*, Cropsey refers to Smith's acknowledgments of the defects of commercial society as "tokens of his [Smith's] regret," and on page 92 to Smith's "curious ambivalence" on the issue.

[8]In this connection see M. Nussbaum's comments on Smith, distributive justice, and compassion in "Compassion: the Basic Social Emotion," in *Social*

Philosophy and Policy 13 (1996): 27–58. Smith is, however, skeptical about how far we can depend on compassion to produce beneficence outside our circles of sympathy (e.g., VI.ii.1.21). Were compassion exercised "locally" but in a sustained way, in part through the kinds of institutions Smith praises (e.g., religious sects), it might nonetheless have a significant social impact.

[9]The sense of merit is a "compounded sentiment" consisting of approval of the sentiments of the agent and of the gratitude of the beneficiaries of his actions, whether or not the beneficiaries actually feel the gratitude they ought. Smith speaks here of our acting the part, in our imaginations, of the actor in a scene of benevolence or justice, and reaching our various judgments accordingly (II.i.5.2, 3).

[10]For a detailed analysis of Smith's jurisprudence, and especially of the *Lectures on Jurisprudence*, see Haakonssen's *The Science of a Legislator*, chs. 5–7.

[11]The dividing line between duties of beneficence and justice is not always clear; an obvious case concerns the duties of parents toward their children. Smith acknowledges that in such cases, the sovereign may "command mutual good offices to a certain degree," but "of all the duties of a law-giver, however, this, perhaps, is that which it requires the greatest delicacy and reserve to execute with propriety and judgment." We are not surprised by the emphasis on judgment, nor on Smith's presumption in favor of the notion that relations of beneficence are free. To go too far in extorting beneficence is "destructive of all liberty, security, and justice" (II.ii.1.8).

[12]Admittedly the connection between the "pungency" of pain and the precision of the general rules of justice is somewhat obscure. As Haakonssen notes, Smith does not spell out the connection (*The Science of a Legislator*, p. 86). I suspect the full answer would bring together a nexus of different ideas. Part of the explanation may lie in the *urgency* the spectator feels to respond to pain. To take a relatively straightforward example, the sight of a child being beaten requires of the decent spectator a swift and certain response whose proportionality to the crime must be precisely fixed on the spot. An equality between the pain endured and the pain inflicted as punishment on the perpetrator seems a necessity (both emotive and prudential) of the spectator's response, and this equality must generally be stated precisely (just this much punishment for just that crime). By contrast, however much and however easily the spectator may participate in a child's joy in, say, a new toy, the spectator presumably and rightly feels no urgency to further that joy right away and to just such and such a degree.

[13]Notice that justice is tied closely to *actions*; this grows out of the starting point in resentment for harm done. An action causes harm in a sense in which a mere intention, or sentiment, or thought of an action generally does not. Notice too that at this founding and basic level, the actions are directed by individuals toward or against other individuals. This is reinforced by the insistence that the proper object of our gratitude or resentment be capable not

just of intentionally causing but also of feeling the sensations of pleasure and pain (II.iii.1.6). Of course, the *administration* of (commutative) justice is obviously a political and jurisprudential matter, and its fairness can be evaluated. But Smith's account makes it clear that the original and primary context of our passions and sympathetic imagination concerns individuals. They are the fundamental moral units; it is the harms and benefits to them that weigh most heavily in the sympathetic imagination.

[14]This is more or less what V. Brown concludes in *Adam Smith's Discourse; The Theory of Moral Sentiments"* moral system "excluded the development of a political personality, and accorded a lower moral status to the public as opposed to the private virtues" (pp. 211–12). I find this only partially true at best.

[15]See VI.ii.intro.2, VI.iii.11; VII.iv.8, 9; III.5.2, III.6.10; II.ii.1.10, II.ii.2.2, 3; VII.ii.intro.2; *The Wealth of Nations* I.x.c.12. This vocabulary is remarkable in an author whose views about religion are rather skeptical.

[16]Consider Smith's pronouncement in *The Wealth of Nations* that "the property which every man has in his own labour, as it is the original foundation of all other property, so it is the most sacred and inviolable." To deprive a "poor man" from deploying his strength and ability in whatever way he thinks best, so long as he does no injury to his neighbour, "is a plain violation of this most sacred property" and an "encroachment upon the just liberty" of the individual (I.x.c.12). While Smith shows in *The Wealth of Nations* that public measures and individuals encroach in this way—sometimes intentionally and sometimes not—a just person will certainly protest them. Smith himself does protest them, by publishing the *The Wealth of Nations.*

[17]Smith in effect presents us with an empirical version of Kant's notion of the moral law as a "fact of reason," there are also crucial differences present as well.

[18]I owe this term to Stephen Darwall's "Sympathetic Liberalism: Recent Work on Adam Smith," *Philosophy and Public Affairs* 28 (1999): 139–64.

[19]I spell out the argument at length in my *Adam Smith and the Virtues of Enlightenment* (Cambridge and New York: Cambridge University Press, 1999), ch. 7.

[20]Just how would have been explained in detail in missing parts of Smith's *corpus.* Once again, I refer the reader to K. Haakonssen's *The Science of a Legislator* for discussion.

[21]Consider *The Wealth of Nations* IV.viii.30: "To hurt in any degree the interest of any one order of citizens, for no other purpose but to promote that of some other, is evidently contrary to that justice and equality of treatment which the sovereign owes to all the different orders of his subjects." Cf. the reference at *The Wealth of Nations* IV.ix.3. to "the liberal plan of equality, liberty, and justice."

[22]His clear headed realism is evident in many places, e.g., *The Wealth of Nations* V.i.b.12: "Civil government, so far as it is instituted for the security of property, is in reality instituted for the defense of the rich against the poor, or of those who have some property against those who have none at all."

[23]For example, as to what type of labor is more likely to yield value, Smith comments: "each individual, it is evident, can, in his local situation, judge much better than any statesman or lawgiver can do for him. The statesman, who should attempt to direct private people in what manner they ought to employ their capitals, would not only load himself with a most unnecessary attention, but assume an authority which could safely be trusted, not only to no single person, but to no council or senate whatever, and which would nowhere be so dangerous as in the hands of a man who had folly and presumption enough to fancy himself fit to exercise it" (*The Wealth of Nations* IV.ii.10). See also *The Wealth of Nations* II.iii.36: "It is the highest impertinence and presumption, therefore, in kings and ministers, to pretend to watch over the economy of private people . . . ." And T*he Wealth of Nations* IV.v.b.16: "But the law ought always to trust people with the care of their own interest, as in their local situations they must generally be able to judge better of it than the legislator can do." See also the references to the limits of "human wisdom" at *The Wealth of Nations* I.ii.1; IV.vii.b.21; IV.vii.c.80; and III.iv.17.

[24]In his own voice he declares that "I have no great faith in political arithmetick" (*The Wealth of Nations* IV.v.b.30); and "I have never known much good done by those who affected to trade for the publick good" (*The Wealth of Nations* IV.ii.9).

[25]*The Wealth of Nations* IV.iii.c.9. Cf. V.i.g.19 and the reference to "management and persuasion" as the "easiest and the safest instruments of government."

[26]Consider Hume's comments about distributive justice in *The Enquiry Concerning the Principles of Morals*, pp. 192–94. Smith must have known those comments.

[27]They also include proportionally higher taxes on luxury vehicles so that the "indolence and vanity of the rich is made to contribute in a very easy manner to the relief of the poor" (V.i.d.5; cf. V.i.d.13), backed up by observations that it is not "unreasonable" for the rich to contribute proportionally more than do the poor to public expences (V.ii.e.6) and by strenuous objections to taxation that supports "inequality of the worst kind" (that in which the poor bear a heavier burden than the rich; V.ii.e.16–19). For discussion of other examples, see N. Rosenberg's "Some Institutional Aspects of *The Wealth of Nations*," *Journal of Political Economy* 68 (1960): 361–74.

[28]For discussion of Smith and the corn laws, see Winch's *Riches and Poverty* (Cambridge: Cambridge University Press, 1996), pp. 205–9. I am much in agreement with Winch's remarks in this book about Smith's view of distributive justice (pp. 97–103).

[29]For example, we read at *The Wealth of Nations* IV.ix.17: "it can never be the interest of the unproductive class to oppress the other two classes [the "cultivators" and the "proprietors"]. . . . The establishment of perfect justice, of perfect liberty, and of perfect equality, is the very simple secret which most effectually secures the highest degree of prosperity to all the three classes." It does not follow that one could not have a degree of prosperity without free-

dom. See D. Forbes, "Sceptical Whiggism, Commerce and Liberty," in A. S. Skinner and T. Wilson, eds., *Essays on Adam Smith* (Oxford: Oxford University Press, 1975), p. 201.

[30]I note that Smith's impartial spectator approves of the "bourgeois" virtue of prudence, though perhaps accords it only "cold esteem" (*The Theory of Moral Sentiments* VI.i.14).

[31]*The Wealth of Nations* insists that "the desire of bettering our condition" is one that "comes with us from the womb, and never leaves us till we go into the grave. Smith continues: "In the whole interval which separates those two moments, there is scarce perhaps a single instant in which any man is so perfectly and completely satisfied with his situation, as to be without any wish of alteration or improvement, of any kind. An augmentation of fortune is the means by which the greater part of men propose and wish to better their condition. It is the means the most vulgar and the most obvious" (*The Wealth of Nations* II.iii.28). "Vulgar" certainly reiterates *The Theory of Moral Sentiments'* qualified disapprobation of the ordinary desire to better our condition. Cf. *The Theory of Moral Sentiments* IV.1.10.

[32]Smith writes of the worker or one of the "laboring poor" doomed to repetitive operations that he "generally becomes as stupid and ignorant as it is possible for a human creature to become. The torpor of his mind renders him, not only incapable of relishing or bearing a part in any rational conversation, but of conceiving any generous, noble, or tender sentiment, and consequently of forming any just judgment concerning many even of the ordinary duties of private life." *The Wealth of Nations* V.i.f.50. Smith follows this rhetorical explosion with a forceful statement of the paradox: "His dexterity at his own particular trade seems, in this manner, to be acquired at the expence of his intellectual, social, and martial virtues" (*The Wealth of Nations* V.i.f.50). Passages similar to those in the *The Wealth of Nations* may be found in *Lectures on Jurisprudence* (B)333: "These are the disadvantages of a commercial spirit. The minds of men are contracted and rendered incapable of elevation, education is despised or at least neglected, and heroic spirit is almost utterly extinguished. To remedy these defects would be an object worthy of serious attention." It is easy to see why Marx was, as one commentator says, "fond of quoting from these passages," and that they may be a source of Marx's notion of "alienation." For both of the thoughts in this sentence, see R. L. Meek's *Smith, Marx, and After: Ten Essays in the Development of Economic Thought* (London: Chapman and Hall, 1977), p. 14. The urgency of the matter is evident in his remarks that "In free countries, where the safety of government depends very much upon the favourable judgment which the people may form of its conduct, it must surely be of the highest importance that they should not be disposed to judge rashly or capriciously it" (*The Wealth of Nations* V.i.f.61).

[33]I refer to J. Gray's *Enlightenment's Wake: Politics and Culture at the Close of the Modern Age* (New York: Routledge, 1995). I discuss the book in detail in my review of the book, *Political Theory* 27 (1999): 274–81.

[34]The quoted phrase is K. Haakonssen's. See his "Jurisprudence and Politics in Adam Smith," in *Traditions of Liberalism*, K. Haakonssen, ed. (St. Leonards, Australia: The Centre for Independent Studies, 1988), p. 112. Among many passages touching on the matter of imperfection, one finds: "What institution of government could tend so much to promote the happiness of mankind as the general prevalence of wisdom and virtue? All government is but an imperfect remedy for the deficiency of these" (*The Theory of Moral Sentiments* IV.2.1).

[35]Smith remarks that "All systems either of preference or of restraint, therefore, being thus completely taken away, the obvious and simple system of natural liberty establishes itself of its own accord" (*The Wealth of Nations* IV.ix.51).

[36]A longer and somewhat different version of this essay was presented at a conference on April 17, 1999, at the University of Paris, and yet another version was presented on July 8, 2002, at the Siemens Stiftung (Munich). The present version was presented at Hillsdale College (MI) on February 4, 2003.

The bulk of this essay is drawn, with a variety of changes, from the unedited manuscript of my *Adam Smith and the Virtues of Enlightenment* (Cambridge: Cambridge University Press, 1999). I am grateful to Cambridge University Press for permission to draw from the book. The reader there will find a more extensive account of Smith's theories.

Lucas E. Morel

Locke, Lincoln, and American Capitalism

It has been said that sometimes the best debates take place among those of one's own political persuasion, and this looks to be the case for economics, as well. It certainly is the case for the study of Lincoln.

In 1994, University of Virginia Professor Merrill Peterson wrote *Lincoln in American Memory*. In this definitive history of Lincoln's public image, Peterson sketches five portraits of Lincoln that have taken hold of the popular imagination: Lincoln as (1) Savior of the Union, (2) Great Emancipator, (3) Man of the People, (4) First American, and (5) Self-Made Man. Which one is the real or most representative Lincoln? Peterson writes: "The public remembrance of the past, as differentiated from the historical scholars', is concerned less with establishing its truth than with appropriating it for the present."[1] My task can be seen as a combination of both objectives: to establish the truth about Lincoln on the subject of Locke and American capitalism for purposes of a contemporary lecture series on economics.

"Appropriating" Lincoln for the cause of capitalism, it so happens, is not too difficult a task, especially given the focus of his earliest years in the political arena. Books like Gabor Boritt's *Lincoln and the Economics of the American Dream* (1978), Daniel Walker Howe's *The Political Culture of the American Whigs* (1979), Allen Guelzo's *Abraham Lincoln: Redeemer President* (1999), and most recently Stewart Winger's *Lincoln, Religion, and Romantic Cultural Politics* (2003) all show how much political economy drove Lincoln's early political agenda.

Still, among the thousands of books on Lincoln that have been published, no one has yet to title a book "Lincoln the Capitalist." And for

101

good reason, as this would limit Lincoln's importance to America. This, in fact, shows a core insight into Lincoln's greatness: namely, his refusal to set his personal and public horizons on merely an economic basis—a basis he very much believed in, but only as the context or environment for other, more lofty individual and social goals.

Simply put, *Lincoln understood the principles of American capitalism in light of the natural rights that support it.* The touchstone for this view was the Declaration of Independence. Lincoln said he "never had a feeling politically that did not spring from the sentiments embodied in the Declaration of Independence." He called it "the charter of our liberties" and its consent principle "the sheet anchor of American republicanism."[2]

This made him not only a student of Thomas Jefferson—at least as far as natural right goes, if not party practice—and of the American founders, in general, but also of that premier philosopher of the Enlightenment, John Locke. Locke first became famous with his book *An Essay Concerning Human Understanding* (1690). But he is most commonly known today for his *Two Treatises of Civil Government* (published anonymously in the same year), the second of which the American founders used to great rhetorical effect in their fight for independence.

For our purposes, I will focus on the fifth chapter of John Locke's *Second Treatise of Civil Government,* one of the longest and most pivotal of the book. It examines private property and the labor that brings it into being. What some have called the "labor theory of value" is on full display here, not so much as an economic theory but as a way of bringing the property question to the political foreground. Locke argued that the protection of property was the *summum bonum* of civil society; there is no security for the fruit of one's labor in the state of nature, where one must fend for oneself in a world without government. The individual thus leaves his natural state by forming a compact with others and establishing civil government to remedy the defects of the state of nature: namely, (1) no known law, (2) no impartial judge, and (3) no due execution of punishment. For Locke, self-preservation was the prime directive of human life, which meant preserving one's life entailed preserving one's liberty and property.

With a deft use of biblical references and rational argument, Locke maintains that because an individual has "a property in his own person" and in the "labour of his body, and the work of his hands," he therefore owns the product of his labor. Whatever "he hath mixed his labour with" he "thereby makes it his property." Locke goes on to argue that "God gave the world . . . to the use of the industrious and rational, (and labour was to be his title to it)." He also makes "the invention of money" of signal importance to the development of the earth's resources, for without it—something that does not perish or go to waste in exchange for things that do—the individual has little incentive beyond mere subsistence to work hard, both physically and mentally, to improve his or her lot in life. Locke calls this "invention and arts," which are necessary to provide "the conveniences of life." Locke wrote that "different degrees of industry were apt to give men possessions in different proportions," which the invention of money and the liberation of acquisition from traditional strictures against greed, gave full effect. We can now see why Locke called the chief end of civil society "the preservation of property," for with the protection of one's life, liberty, and property, one was able to provide a commodious living free of the dangers attendant to man's natural state.[3]

Now, we have no clear evidence that Lincoln actually read any of Locke's writings. The most authoritative scholarship on the subject, Douglas Wilson's *Herndon's Informants* (1997) and *Honor's Voice* (1998), contains no reference to Locke. But as Lincoln's references to Henry Clay, Thomas Jefferson, and the Declaration of Independence indicate, at minimum he got his Locke honestly through individuals and writings shaped by Locke. What are the key elements of Locke's political economy just described, and how do we see these at work in Lincoln's political theory and practice? I will highlight seven, focusing on some more than others, and then look at Lincoln's view of the relationship between labor and capital in particular.

First, and foremost, Lincoln believed in the equality of human rights. As the Declaration of Independence puts it, "We hold these truths to be self-evident, that all men are created equal. That they are endowed by their Creator with certain inalienable rights; that among these are life, liberty, and the pursuit of happiness." This is a gloss on Locke's *Second Treatise*, which states that each individual is entitled to his or her "life, liberty, and property" (cf. Locke's *An Essay Concerning Human Understanding*, which discusses the "pursuit of happiness" in the context of individual power and thought).

Lincoln stated that "each man should do precisely as he pleases with all which is exclusively his own," and called this the "foundation" of his own "sense of justice." At the core of this equality, the "birth-right" of all people, was individual freedom. "Liberty to all," Lincoln wrote, is "the principle that clears the path for all—gives hope to all—and, by consequence, *enterprize*, and *industry* to all." This individ-ual liberty would ineluctably produce private property. If, as Lincoln wrote, "the individual has some natural right to himself," then he also has the right to the fruit of his labor. In short, the right to private property derives from the right to one's own liberty.[4]

This principle went down so deep for Lincoln that in the 1858 debates with U.S. Senator Stephen Douglas, an election campaign where no blacks were allowed to vote, Lincoln still insisted that blacks were "entitled to the natural rights enumerated in the Declaration of Independence." He continued: "in the right to eat the bread, with-out the leave of anybody else, which his own hand earns, he is my equal, and the equal of Judge Douglas, and the equal of every living man." (Note Lincoln's allusion to Genesis 3:19.)[5] The principle of "Liberty to all" is at the core of the Declaration of Independence, the chief end of the American struggle for self-government, and what Lincoln called "the primary cause of our great prosperity."[6]

But for liberty to be exercised and enjoyed, and to produce not just subsistence but prosperity, it needs protection. Which brings us to the second Lockean principle to which Lincoln was devoted: Gov-ernment exists to secure rights. Lincoln told a regiment of soldiers that they were fighting to perpetuate what he called "this great and free government," which gave "an open field and a fair chance for your industry, enterprise and intelligence: that you may all have equal privileges in the race of life, with all its desirable aspirations."[7]

Here, government exists to "secure" what people already pos-sess, the equal rights to "life, liberty, and the pursuit of happiness." As Lincoln put it, "To [secure] to each labourer the whole product of his labour, or as nearly as possible, is a most worthy object of any good government." And if government did its job well, the natural equality of men would express itself in the development of their indi-vidual capacities. As Lincoln put it, "Advancement—improvement in condition is the order of things in a society of equals."[8]

The third Lockean principle in Lincoln's political theory is gov-ernment by consent of the governed—"no man is good enough to

govern another man, without that other's consent"—"this is the leading principle—the sheet anchor of American republicanism." What
Lincoln called "our ancient faith" was a rejection of a more ancient
faith that posited a "divine right of kings," which the American
founders threw off most explicitly in their Declaration of Independence.[9] As Thomas Jefferson wrote near the end of his life: "the mass
of mankind has not been born with saddles on their backs, nor a
favored few booted and spurred, ready to ride them legitimately."[10]

The fourth Lockean/Lincolnian principle is limited government. The Constitution, as a federal form of government, vests limited powers in the three branches of the national government. This
was always Lincoln's understanding, and one he reiterated at the
outset of his First Inaugural Address as it pertained to slavery in the
South: "I have no purpose, directly or indirectly, to interfere with the
institution of slavery in the States where it exists. I believe I have no
lawful right to do so."[11] The Constitution restricted what Lincoln as
president could do about the "peculiar institution," and as the most
deliberate and settled will of the American people, the constitution
stood as the political lodestar for Lincoln.

The fifth Lockean principle Lincoln preached and practiced was
the rule of law. He explained this principle at length in his 1838 Lyce-
um Address at Springfield. He applied this principle in his political
approach to the existence of slavery, especially his effort to prevent its
extension and most famously in his monumental war measure, the
Emancipation Proclamation.[12]

Lincoln connects the rule of law to property rights in his reply
to the New York Workingmen's Democratic Republican Association,
where he called "the existing rebellion" a "war upon the rights of all
working people." An emphasis upon "all working people" might be
in order, given that Lincoln replied specifically to their comments
about southern secession as tending to more than a "perpetuation of
African slavery." Simply put, slavery stood as the clearest subversion
of the rights of working people, and Lincoln subsumed the plight of
the enslaved African within that of working men everywhere.[13]

In addition to quoting verbatim from his first state of the union address, which detailed his view of the relationship between labor and capital, Lincoln went on to close his reply with an exhortation against envy:

That some should be rich, shows that others may become rich, and hence is just encouragement to industry and enterprize. Let not him who is houseless pull down the house of another; but let him labor diligently and build one for himself, thus by example assuring that his own shall be safe from violence when built.[14]

The previous year, just a few days after the victorious Gettysburg campaign, New York experienced a draft riot that killed over a hundred and burned or looted businesses (a bowdlerized version of which, I am told, you can see in the latest Martin Scorsese film, *Gangs of New York*). Not envy, but aspiration, should be one's response to the prosperity of others. The security of property rights, both in law and public sentiment, was essential to the development of American capitalism.[15]

The sixth Lockean principle found in Lincoln's political thought was the right of revolution. In an 1848 speech against President James Polk's precipitation of the Mexican War, Lincoln endorsed the right of revolution: "Any people . . . have the *right* to rise up and shake off the existing government." He called it "a right which, we hope and believe, is to liberate the world." However, in his First Inaugural Address of 1861, he was careful to distinguish this right from southern secession, which did not claim as its basis the individual right to self-government but rather a state's right to withdraw from its obligations to the union of American states under the U.S. Constitution.[16]

The seventh Lockean principle found in Lincoln's statesmanship is the executive prerogative. This was exemplified in actions he took while Congress was out of session in the first few months of the Civil War. Congress retroactively affirmed his actions as legitimate (except for one, the president's suspension of the privilege of the writ of habeas corpus), arising from the urgency of a rebellion requiring the president to act in Congress' absence. In his July 4, 1861, speech before a special session of Congress, Lincoln explained that he "believed that nothing has been done beyond the constitutional competency of Congress."[17] This explanation fits Locke's definition of prerogative as "a power, in the hands of the prince, to provide for the public good, in such cases, which depending upon unforeseen and uncertain occurrences, certain and unalterable laws could not safely direct."[18] Defending the nation from violent secession required prudence of the highest order. Thus, Lincoln the president followed Locke the political philosopher in exercising his constitutional prerogative to "do so much as may seem to be required by the public safety"[19] and thereby fulfill the great political adage—*Salus populi suprema lex* ("the good of the people is the supreme law").

With this background on the Lockean political principles informing Lincoln's political theory and practice, we now turn to Lincoln's view of the role capitalism plays in a free society.

Lincoln presents his most direct examination of the relationship between labor and capital in his first state of the union address in December 1861. (He had first made this argument at a Wisconsin Agricultural Fair in 1859.)[20] He said:

> Labor is prior to, and independent of, capital. Capital is only the fruit of labor, and could never have existed if labor had not first existed. Labor is the superior of capital, and deserves much the higher consideration. Capital has its rights, which are as worthy of protection as any other rights. Nor is it denied that there is, and probably always will be, a relation between labor and capital, producing mutual benefits. The error is in assuming that the whole labor of community exists within that relation. A few men own capital, and that few avoid labor themselves, and, with their capital, hire or buy another few to labor for them. A large majority belong to neither class—neither work for others, nor have others working for them. In most of the southern States, a majority of the whole people of all colors are neither slaves nor masters; while in the northern a large majority are neither hirers nor hired. Men with their families—wives, sons, and daughters—work for themselves, on their farms, in their houses, and in their shops, taking the whole product to themselves, and asking no favors of capital on the one hand, nor of hired laborers or slaves on the other. It is not forgotten that a considerable number of persons mingle their own labor with capital—that is, they labor with their own hands, and also buy or hire others to labor for them; but this is only a mixed, and not a distinct class. No principle stated is disturbed by the existence of this mixed class.
>
> Again: as has already been said, there is not, of necessity, any such thing as the free hired laborer being fixed to that condition for life. Many independent men everywhere in these

States, a few years back in their lives, were hired laborers. The prudent, penniless beginner in the world, labors for wages awhile, saves a surplus with which to buy tools or land for himself; then labors on his own account another while, and at length hires another new beginner to help him. This is the just, and generous, and prosperous system, which opens the way to all— gives hope to all, and consequent energy, and progress, and improvement of condition to all.[21]

A year before his first inauguration as president, Lincoln said: "I want every man to have the chance—and I believe a black man is entitled to it—in which he can better his condition, when he may look forward and hope to be a hired laborer this year and the next, work for himself afterward, and finally to hire men to work for him. That is the true system."[22] Simply put, Lincoln believed in labor prior to capital, or as he said elsewhere "the man before the dollar." Now, was Lincoln a "free trader"? Of utmost concern to Lincoln was that a worker receive the maximum return on his effort—the full fruit of his labor. As noted earlier, Locke thought waste was a form of theft from the community, a removal of too much from what was held in common that could no longer be consumed by someone else: "As much as anyone can make use of to any advantage of life before it spoils, so much he may by his labour fix a property in: whatever is beyond this, is more than his share, and belongs to others."[23]

Lincoln followed a version of this: to wit, "The man who produces a good full crop will scarcely ever let any part of it go to waste." Lincoln argued that what a person does well, he is proud of and takes care of: "Thus, he labors with satisfaction, and saves to himself the whole fruit of his labor."[24] Applying this to international trade, Lincoln's emphasis was not so much what was lost to others through waste, but what was lost to the worker himself in producing a surplus intended for sale but whose proceeds were eaten up by the costs associated with getting the product to distant buyers.

For example, what we call "free trade" was to Lincoln hardly free. He argued, in typical Whig fashion, that the costs of exporting goods—namely, transportation, insurance, storage, and other "middleman" activities that Lincoln called "useless labour"—devalued or eroded the original effort that produced the goods for sale. Lincoln wrote that "all labour done *directly* and *incidentally* in *carrying* articles to their place of consumption, which could have been produced in sufficient abundance, *with as little labour, at the place of consumption*, as at the place they were carried from, is useless labour."[25]

This is why he believed the freest trade was that done close to home. He therefore favored state and federal support for "internal improvements"—for example, roads, canals, railroads, and bridges— to assist both manufacturers and farmers in getting their goods to market within the United States. This also explains Lincoln's support for protectionist tariffs, especially on luxury items, which were not necessary for the great mass of society. These tariffs would help pay for internal improvements, and help "infant industries" get established at home, thereby developing national self-sufficiency and providing a greater diversity of work opportunities for the growing American population.[26] This diversity of employment, akin to the division of labor and specialization, would enable more individuals labor at that which they were both good at and proud of.

Connected with this is his support for a national banking system, not merely to collect these tariffs but to provide a stable and reliable currency. This would assist, again, the small farmer and cottage industrialist by ensuring that the value of monetary script would not fluctuate too greatly by the time their wares made it to market. Farmers and artisans would have little incentive to seek greater access to buyers not close to home if their investment in selling their goods evaporated by the time their products got to market and were bought with inflated dollars.

Lincoln did acknowledge that "the greatest real objection to improvements" was the charge of its "*Particularity*": namely, "expending the money of the *whole* people for an object which will benefit only a *portion* of them." He simply did not believe that federal money for what he called "a general system of improvements" was unconstitutional because the nation as a whole would benefit.[27] This followed from his definition of government:

> The legitimate object of government, is to do for a community of people, whatever they need to have done, but can not do, *at*

all, or can not, *so well do*, for themselves —in their separate, and individual capacities.

In all that the people can individually do as well for themselves, government ought not to interfere.[28]

He went on to say that the objects of government not related to"wrongs" or criminal punishment included "all which, in its nature, and without wrong, requires combined action, as public roads and highways, public schools, charities, pauperism, orphanage, estates of the deceased, and the machinery of government itself."[29]

This Whig political economy, championed by Lincoln's "beau ideal of a statesman," Henry Clay, was known as the "American System."[30] It also served to counter Democratic expansionism, the desire for new territories, which Lincoln and fellow Whigs resisted. For example, Lincoln wrote that he "never was much interested in the Texas question"—that is, the American annexation of Texas. However, he confessed that if annexation could be shown to "augment the evil of slavery" by "find[ing] new places for it to live in," when it could no longer live in the old, then Lincoln argued, "we should never knowingly lend ourselves directly or indirectly, to prevent that slavery from dying a natural death."[31]

Lincoln's political reason for being was wholly connected to preserving the Constitution as it was understood by those who framed it: "I am exceedingly anxious that this Union, the Constitution, and the liberties of the people shall be perpetuated in accordance with the original idea for which that struggle was made." He continued, "And I shall be most happy indeed if I shall be an humble instrument in the hands of the Almighty, and of this, his almost chosen people, for perpetuating the object of that great struggle." In other words, it was not just saving the Union, but saving it, as he put it, "as to make, and to keep it, forever worthy of the saving."[32]

This requires a certain understanding of the American regime, a devotion to its principles of the equal rights of humanity. Keep sight of this, and Americans will be able, in the words of Lincoln, to "rise up to the height of a generation of men worthy of a free Government."[33]

Notes

[1] Merrill D. Peterson, *Lincoln in American Memory* (New York: Oxford University Press, 1994), p. 35.

[2] *Abraham Lincoln: His Speeches and Writings*, Roy P. Basler, ed. (Cleveland: World Pub. Co., 1946), pp. 577; 403; 304.

[3] John Locke, *Second Treatise of Civil Government*, C. B. Macpherson, ed. (Indianapolis: Hackett Publishing Company, Inc., 1980), chapter 5.

[4] *Abraham Lincoln: His Speeches and Writings*, pp. 303 & 394; 757; 513. [Emphases in original.]

[5] Genesis 3:19 reads: "In the sweat of thy face shalt thou eat bread, till thou return unto the ground; for out of it was thou taken: for dust thou art, and unto dust shalt thou return." Lincoln understood this verse to describe the lot of all human beings, which meant that if some individuals forced others to work for them without recompense, they were not only stealing, but also attempting to avoid the dictates of the Almighty. Material acquisition was only one component of life on earth. For some individuals to make acquisition an end secured by the enslavement of others would be, in Lincoln's mind, "a dangerous dalliance" and "a sad evidence that, feeling prosperity, we forget right." (*Abraham Lincoln: His Speeches and Writings*, p. 313.) This would undermine respect for the liberty that gave rise to prosperity—a liberty that all individuals possess by nature and hence deserve to have protected equally.

[6] *Abraham Lincoln: His Speeches and Writings*, pp. 445; 513.

[7] Ibid., pp. 756–57.

[8] *Collected Works of Abraham Lincoln*, Roy P. Basler, ed. (New Brunswick, NJ: Rutgers University Press, 1953), 1:412; 3:462.

[9] *Abraham Lincoln: His Speeches and Writings*, pp. 304; 308.

[10] June 24, 1826, Letter to Roger C. Weightman, *The Portable Thomas Jefferson*, Merrill D. Peterson, ed. (New York: Viking Penguin, Inc., 1975), p. 575; also see Harry Jaffa, *A New Birth of Freedom: Abraham Lincoln and the Coming of the Civil War* (Lanham, MD: Rowman & Littlefield Publishers, Inc., 2000), pp. 111–12.

[11] *Abraham Lincoln: His Speeches and Writings*, p. 580. Near the end of his inaugural address, Lincoln remarked, "By the frame of the government under which we live, this same people have wisely given their public servants but little power for mischief; and have, with equal wisdom, provided for the return of that little to their own hands at very short intervals" (pp. 587–88).

[12] For Lincoln's statesmanship as applied to the problem of slavery, see Allen C. Guelzo, *Lincoln's Emancipation Proclamation: The End of Slavery in America* (New York: Simon & Schuster, 2004); and George Anastoplo, *Abraham Lincoln: A Constitutional Biography* (Lanham, MD: Rowman & Littlefield Publishers, Inc., 1999), chap. 14, "Emancipation Proclamation." Cf. Lerone Bennett, Jr., *Forced*

Into Glory: Abraham Lincoln's White Dream (Chicago: Johnson Publishing Company, 1999); and my review of Bennett's book: Lucas Morel, "Forced into Gory Lincoln Revisionism," *Claremont Review of Books* (Fall 2000).

[13] *Collected Works of Abraham Lincoln*, 7:259.

[14] Ibid., 7:259–60.

[15] See Thomas G. West, *Vindicating the Founders: Race, Sex, Class, and Justice in the Origins of America* (Lanham, MD: Rowman & Littlefield Publishers, Inc., 1997), chap. 2, "Property Rights."

[16] *Abraham Lincoln: His Speeches and Writings*, pp. 209 [emphasis in original]; 584–85.

[17] Ibid, p. 600.

[18] Locke, *Second Treatise of Government*, pp. 83; 81. For Locke's explication of prerogative in general, see his *Second Treatise of Government*, chaps. 13–14. For a modern assessment of executive prerogative, see Harvey C. Mansfield, Jr., *Taming the Prince: The Ambivalence of Modern Executive Power* (Baltimore: The Johns Hopkins University Press, 1993; orig. publ. The Free Press, 1989), chap. 8.

[19] *Abraham Lincoln: His Speeches and Writings*, pp. 708. For Lincoln's defense of using martial law in the arrest of Peace Democratic Congressman Clement Vallandingham, see the entire "Letter to Erastus Corning and Others," June 13, 1863, in *Abraham Lincoln: His Speeches and Writings*, pp. 699–708. For Lincoln's presidential policies with regard to civil liberties during the Civil War, see Mark E. Neely, Jr., *The Fate of Liberty: Abraham Lincoln and Civil Liberties* (Oxford University Press, 1991), and more generally on Lincoln's political prudence, see Harry V. Jaffa, *A New Birth of Freedom: Abraham Lincoln and the Coming of the Civil War* (Lanham, MD: Rowman & Littlefield Publishers, Inc., 2000).

[20] *Abraham Lincoln: His Speeches and Writings*, pp. 500–502.

[21] *Collected Works of Abraham Lincoln*, 5:52.

[22] Ibid., 4:24.

[23] *Abraham Lincoln: His Speeches and Writings*, pp. 489; 488; 20–21.

[24] Ibid., p. 497.

[25] *Collected Works of Abraham Lincoln*, 1:412.

[26] See Daniel Walker Howe, *The Political Culture of the American Whigs* (Chicago: The University of Chicago Press, 1979), chap. 5, "The Entrepreneurial Ethos."

[27] *Abraham Lincoln: His Speeches and Writings*, p. 238. [Emphases in original.]

[28] *Collected Works of Abraham Lincoln*, 2:220. [Emphases in original.]

[29] Ibid., 2:221.

[30] See Howe, chap. 6, "Henry Clay, Ideologue of the Center."

[31] *Abraham Lincoln: His Speeches and Writings*, p. 170.

[32] Ibid., pp. 575; 315.

[33] Ibid., p. 756.

GEORGE GILDER

Ronald Reagan and the Supply-Side Myth

Once upon a time, eons ago, in an earlier century in a previous millennium, there was a land, somewhere between Nod and N'ere-do-well, in the thrall of a ruthless and unforgiving ruler. Call him Ray-Gun. A mythical horned figure from the plains east of Eden and west of Hillsdale, a bad actor in word and deed, smeared with theatrical makeup, he seized power brandishing a cleaver and a scythe. In the politer circles of Cambridge, Massachusetts, and Georgetown in the District of Columbia, the mere mention of his name would make children clutch their vulnerable body parts and dogs and cats scramble for the protection of PETA.

Under the cloud of his oppressive regime, the entire intelligentsia began to blither unintelligibly. Eminent social scientists and professors of refined arts from leading universities found their minds freeze and tongues swell as they responded to every query by mumbling strange mantras, as if in a trance: "Sexism, racism, and homophobia," or "Racism, homism, and sexophobia," they would mutter, or "Tax huts for the rich, tax rich for the cuts, fax sluts for the itch." Or something. What they meant no one knew. Many elite thinkers questioned whether this Ray-Gun had ever been legitimately elected, since they personally had never met anyone who had voted for him.

Apparently thrust into office by an angry mob of Dead White Males, Ronald Reagan in 1981 took the cleaver to government spending and the scythe to taxes. Tax rates went down 25 percent across the board over three years. So bloodthirsty were his spending cuts that his Director of Management and Budget, David Stockman, appeared on the covers of *Newsqueak, Whine,* and other national broadsides flaunting a butcher's knife dripping blood. At the same time, Reagan mobilized brutal and bootless high tech scythes and cleavers against the peaceable land of the hammer and sickle—a quaint haven for family farmers, carpenters, and sensitive intellectuals called the Union of Soviet Socialist Republics.

As all experts agreed, the reduced tax rates had the effect of starving the government of revenues, forcing further cuts in spending which were unfavorably compared in the media, for compassion and generosity, to Stalin's famine policy in the Ukraine.

Under the Reagan regime, as might be expected, the economy foundered and the nation fell deep into the coils of debt. Tycoons spruce in tuxedoes or casual in designer denim minced their way among homeless vagrants sleeping on the sidewalks of New York and on the beaches of Santa Monica. The government budget slid from a level of near surplus under President Carter to a deficit nearing $300 billion under Reagan. Amid a collapsing balance of trade, the private sector was forced to borrow heavily from charitable foreigners. The nation moved from its traditional role as a fatcat creditor to the world under previous civilized presidents to a mendicant plight as global net debtor. Twin towers of debt, they were called—the trade gap and the budget gap—and they meant that vast holdings of American assets, from the links at Pebble Beach and the Rainbow Room at Rockefeller Center to Madonna and Princess Grace, were slipping into the oleaginous hands (or under the balance sheets) of foreigners. As all reputable experts and respectable moral leaders agreed, the debts symbolized an administration that was consuming its "seed corn" and pushing its burdens onto future generations and administrations.

But Reagan just didn't get it, just didn't feel their pain at all. Occasionally on awakening at cabinet meetings to grab and gobble down another handful of jelly beans or deny a petition for clemency from a jaywalker on death row, he would look blithely unconcerned. A stalwart upholder of his own right to bear arms, such as the presidential veto, he responded to plans to reverse his harshest policies by smiling diabolically like a Hollywood killer: "Go ahead, make my day," he memorably snarled (under the guidance of my cousin Josh Gilder).

The nation sunk into a mire of greed and decay, beset with lugubrious media concerns, such as the dire threat to the Constitution posed by some elite chimera called Iran-Contra, which no one could explain without eliciting spontaneous applause for Reagan and Ollie North. Meanwhile, it was alleged, Japan moved to take the lead in high technology—in microchips, computers, automobiles, even aerospace. Peter Drucker declared: "Making memory chips in the U.S. is like growing pineapples in North Dakota." Sages in Washington and on elite university campuses predicted a future of decline and poverty for Americans, possibly preceded by a brief reprieve "flipping hamburgers" and "wringing laundry" for the Japanese, until they managed to automate these menial tasks as well. During this period, I conducted some fifty debates with Ivy League illuminati such as Lester Thurow, Robert Reich, John Kenneth Galbraith, Kevin Phillips, and, on a couple of memorable occasions, Edward Luttwak. They all foresaw the decline and fall of America as an inevitable fate that could be forestalled only by raising tax rates sharply and shoveling federal dollars into the widening maw between rich and poor.

As I said, this is a mythical picture of the Reagan administration. It is a caricature. Yet the strange and ironic fact is that most conservatives believe it in one way or another. That is, they accept the notion that (1) Reagan cut taxes, (2) reduced spending, and (3) expanded debt. One prominent group, dominated by so-called moderate Republicans, formed the Concord Coalition to make the argument that huge deficits were endangering the nation's future. Led by former Treasury Secretary "Pete" Peterson and former Senator Warren Rudman, the Concord Coalition believes that tax cuts can only be justified by previous spending cuts. If you are going to cut taxes, you had better cut spending first. Seems to make sense to most people. Key figures in the Coalition were Richard Friedman, Bush's new Chairman of the Council of Economic Advisors and John Snow, the new Secretary of the Treasury. Other Concordites include John McCain and Pete Domenici, worthy Republican Senators. So the Concord influence may even be growing.

Supporting Reagan's tax rate reductions were a movement of economists and journalists called supply siders. I was one of the supply-side leaders, and in 1980 I authored *Wealth & Poverty*, a book which asserted that lower tax rates yield higher tax revenues; it became a worldwide best seller in ten languages. This proposition about taxes was controversial. Ronald Reagan personally gave a copy of *Wealth & Poverty* to Bob Dole, then Majority Leader of the Senate and later a candidate for president. Something of a literary critic, Dole did not appreciate the president's gift. He liked to tell a bad-news, good-news joke. "The bad news: A Greyhound bus drove off a cliff. The good news: It was filled with supply-side economists."

A core symbolic claim of supply-side economics is called the Laffer Curve, after economist Arthur Laffer. It plots tax rates against tax receipts. According to my research, the correct curve shows that except at very low rates, well below 20 percent, higher tax rates tend to reduce long run government income well below the level that it could have attained with lower rates.

The Laffer curve is now widely discredited. Almost no one in the economics profession—even former supply siders themselves— believe it applies to the United States, or believe that it was demonstrated by the Reagan results. Even Reagan's own advisors, such as Martin Anderson, Paul Craig Roberts, and Martin Feldstein, now deny that the Reagan administration expected the tax cuts to pay for themselves. As a result of this defection, President Bush defends his own tax cuts by saying they "allow people to keep and spend their own money." Even Republicans speak of "paying" for tax cuts with spending cuts, and say that the real burden of government on the economy is what it spends rather than how it taxes. Conservatives everywhere agree that what really matters is to cut spending.

Government outlays are heavily oriented toward public services that seemingly benefit the poor and middle classes. But the tax burden is overwhelmingly borne by the rich. After the Reagan cuts, the top 25 percent of families paid 80 percent of the income taxes. The top half paid 94.5 percent of the income taxes. Therefore, as Thurow, Reich, Phillips, Mark Krugman, Hendrick Hertzberg, and a host of other political criers implacably point out, to cut spending in order to pay for tax cuts is regressive. It takes from the poor and middle class in order to give to the rich. The spending cuts deprive the poor of benefits while the tax cuts go to those who earn high enough incomes to pay income taxes. "Tax cuts for the rich" has become a Dem-

ocratic chant, and even this administration has no plausible answer
to the charge. After all, the administration itself acknowledged that
its tax cut would cost $1.6 trillion over ten years. This is one of the
silliest concessions in political history. Why not say a thousand trillion over one hundred years?

If you believe that tax cuts cost money, you imply that current tax
rates do not obstruct economic activity and thus reductions are unnecessary. If you agree that tax cuts reduce government revenues, you cannot defend the cuts effectively in a democracy in which at least one-third
of the voters are directly dependent on government spending for their
livelihoods and most of the rest cherish some government program or
other. Even conservatives want expanded spending on national security. The effort to cut current programs is futile. It is hard enough just
to resist the creation of new programs and entitlements.

In fact, I have a law about this. Gilder's Law ordains that the
more worthless the government spending the more difficult it is to
cut. Conservatives with a well-informed general desire to cut government outlays will be harried and pilloried for greed and callousness.
But all the government bureaucracies are full of feckless social experts, bilingual educators, gender theorists, breath poets, animal
rights lawyers, eco-propagandists, and Marxoid agitators who could
not possibly get an equivalent job in the private sector. What conceivable market role could be found for an enthusiast for polluting good
gasoline with expensive ethanol? What private sector slot could possibly be found for a so-called "performance artist" who smears excrement on her homely nude body in public in the name of art? This
lady will give her life for more government, disguised as noble subsidies for culture and freedom of expression. And all these government beneficiaries have relatives and Congresspersons who will fight
to the end for their sinecures and be acclaimed in the media for their
selflessness and compassion.

The result is predictable. In the end, Republicans who urge cuts
in spending succeed only in retrenching outlays on defense. Clever
people supply ingenious rationales. A leaner defense is more flexible
and better attuned to the new challenge of terrorism. But, according
to Gilder's Law, cuts in defense spending almost always end up attacking muscle, not fat. Gender rights lawyers attached to every unit

will sue if you retrench daycare for female recruits, and Senators defend to the last shadowy ditches of the appropriations process every worthless military base far from any possible theater of battle, and of course veterans hospitals are sacrosanct.

The effort to cut current programs is political suicide for Republicans. The likely result is Democratic victory, higher tax rates, weaker defense, and a larger absolute size of government.

Reagan's genius was to show the way out of this dilemma. Yet nearly all his critics and supporters fail to grasp what truly happened during his administration. Reagan did indeed cut tax rates by 25 percent across the board. He also cut effective taxes on investment. Although he later adjusted the tax codes in ways that demand-siders called "record tax heights," his supply-side convictions prevented him from ever countenancing a rise in the crucial top rates that he reduced from nearly 50 percent to 28 percent during his regime, and that define the horizons of aspiration in the supply-side economy. So Reagan massively cut tax rates. But nothing else in the myth is true.

As a result of the tax rate reductions, federal revenues surged up by one-third or more over seven years and then continued to expand through the 1990s. Add in increased revenues for state and local governments, and reduced charges for unemployment insurance, and Reagan's tax cuts entirely paid for themselves many times over. Following Reagan's example, countries all around the globe cut their own tax rates and as a result could increase their government spending.

The reason this is possible was explained by a World Bank economist, Keith Marsden. In the mid-1980s, he showed that low tax countries increase their spending three times faster than comparable high tax countries. This is because the low tax economies grow six times faster. For most of the period since World War II, the fastest growing economy in the world, with the fastest growth of government spending, was Hong Kong, with a top rate of 16 percent.[1] A study by Jude Wanniski and his colleagues at Polyconomics extended the analysis through the Reagan era, with the same results.[2] In recent years, Ireland, New Zealand, China, and Russia all could massively increase spending after drastic reductions in tax rates. Russia has increased outlays by some 60 percent after enacting a 13 percent flat tax.[3]

Why do I stress government spending, after a long career of attacking it? Because what is crucial is not the absolute level of government but the relative level of government compared to the size of the private sector. In all these countries that enacted tax rate reductions, government either declined or stopped growing as a share of the total economy.

I should confess here that I too have my own preferred forms of government spending. I gain an exquisite sense of moral and esthetic uplift from watching nude performance artists smearing excrement across their bodies. I also want a strong defense and national security posture. By cutting tax rates, Reagan was able to fund a 50 percent increase in defense spending. This expansion of the military was crucial to winning the cold war. For better or for worse, mostly for worse, he also enlarged social spending by some 25 percent. I didn't like it, but without changes in the electorate, it was politically inevitable. Far from expanding debt, however, Reagan reduced it sharply by negotiating a Social Security Commission that extended the age of retirement and cut back the implicit liabilities in the social security program by some six trillion dollars.

Totally dwarfing all the budgetary deficits put together, the Social Security changes radically improved the fiscal position of the government compared the 1970s when real Social Security liabilities doubled. But the 1970s ended with close to a balanced all-governmental budget (minus Social Security) and a balance of payments surplus. The government was apparently in the black, but most of the private sector was in the red, with savings and loans bankrupt and interest rates at over 15 percent.

While the federal budgetary deficit (exclusive of Social Security) swelled under Reagan in absolute terms, the federal debt shrunk sharply as a share of national assets. The private assets of Americans expanded massively, from some $17 trillion to $30 trillion. The stock market nearly tripled. Between 1980 and 1989, real after-tax personal income rose for every group of the population (20 percent over all). After dropping sharply in the late 1970s, the real income of black families per capita rose 19.9 percent.

Far from losing ground in high technology, the U.S. began a 20-year surge of innovation in computers and communications that has made the U.S. the world's dominant source of technical advance and new wealth. Personal computers and networks became central to world economic growth.

Meanwhile, with the top tax rate dropping from 50 percent to 28 percent under Reagan, tax contributions by the top 5 percent of earners rose from 9 percent of the total to 18 percent, while income tax contributions from the bottom 20 percent dropped to 2 percent. With lower rates under Reagan, the top 50 percent paid 94.5 percent of the income taxes. Lower tax rates for the rich resulted in hugely larger tax payments by the rich.

Why then do critics still speak of voodoo economics? Why do even the remaining supply siders insistently deny that lower tax rates pay for themselves with higher revenues? Why does this administration still speak of $1.6 trillion tax cuts and $300 billion stimulus packages, as if it cost money to reduce counterproductive government burdens? One key reason is the totally stultifying grip of the demand-side model on the entire economics community. University and media economists still function like an establishment of flat earth physicists patiently waiting for the ships of supply siders to fall off the edge of the world.

Demand-side economists believe in something called demand or purchasing power. Essentially demand is measured by money. But supply siders know that money is worthless in itself. It has value only because it represents a previous supply of productive services. You can go to Amazon or Barnes & Noble and buy a copy of *Wealth & Poverty* because you (or your parents) have previously earned the money by supplying some good or service that other people valued. The money is significant only as a symbol of that previous contribution. Sure, you might make a purchase by borrowing, but this just shifts the right to use the money from the lender to the borrower. Debt is merely an enforceable promise to supply goods and services in the future.

What matters to the revenues government can collect from citizens is whether conditions are favorable for the creation of value. Supply-sider Jack Kemp has summed it up: "If you want more of something, you subsidize it. If you want less, you tax it."

To be sustained, every economic activity must earn a profit—a surplus above its costs. A business with inadequate revenues or customers to defray its costs may raise its prices. But by raising prices, most businesses with inadequate revenues lose both revenues and customers. Look at Amazon, a company with a profit problem over the last several years. Did it raise prices to compensate? No, Amazon steadily lowered prices, offering a stream of free services, free packaging and mailing, and other benefits. This is the rule of business ever since Henry Ford took over the automobile industry by dropping the price of the Model-T by 60 percent. Expand production, gain economies of scale and learning, and lower prices. This low price strategy has been the hallmark of success of all the high technology businesses that have given the U.S. dominance in the world economy. The best example is the plummeting price of computer power.

Government prices are taxes, which are involuntary. Thus demand siders deny that the low price imperative applies to government. To a demand sider, government seems able to extract wealth from the public whenever it wishes. In an extremity it can merely print money. But the real tax payment is not mere money, which can be multiplied at will by government. The real payment is productive service—work and investment, innovation and creativity—and these productive services are all ultimately voluntary. You can't force someone to invent something or even to work effectively. The government may mandate a payment, but it cannot mandate the productive work, investment, invention, and creativity that are the source of the payment.

To a supply sider, therefore, government is a kind of business. It competes with other governments around the world. It competes to attract taxable businesses and activities to its jurisdiction, and to foster expansion of existing enterprises. To gain tax revenues, governments compete against the rewards of nontaxable activity, such as leisure, barter, early retirement, welfare, crime, and accounting finagles and shelters. To attract taxable activity to its regime, a government should lower its tax rates on additional production.

Remember Amazon and Ford. Like a business with too few customers, a government with inadequate revenues should lower its prices and improve its product. By lowering marginal tax rates—the rates on additional activity—governments can induce people to produce and invest within their borders. By raising tax rates, they drive people to other jurisdictions and to nontaxable activities. That is why high tax rates do not redistribute incomes. They redistribute taxpayers out of taxable activities onto golf courses and barter exchanges and to foreign regimes with lower rates.

A good example was Cuba. Fidel Castro imagined that he could capture the wealth of his island by nationalizing all its businesses. That is the ultimate tax. He aimed to create a great Cuban city in the Western hemisphere. He succeeded. But it was not Havana: It is Miami, where many entrepreneurial Cubans fled. The two million Cubans in the U.S. ended up with a GDP six times higher than what Castro claimed for the six million Cubans in Cuba. A more subtle example is the movement of people and enterprises from high tax California to low tax Nevada next door. It is visible in a town called Incline Village on the edge of Lake Tahoe, which has become one of the three richest jurisdictions in the nation.

Supply-side economics is easy to learn because it is true and the world constantly affirms its truths. Demand-side economics is extremely difficult to master because it gains no long run confirmation from experience. You have to learn stuff like Gini coefficients, investment accelerators, Phillips curves, Gaussian distributions, utility functions, production coefficients, Cobb-Douglas regressions, consumer propensities, money supply indices—M1 through MX—all the multifarious components and permutations of demand, all mostly wrong or misleading. It takes a Ph.D. regime of study to grasp these complexities. Once you have made your way through these demand-side mazes, you do not want to accept the simple truth that Reagan knew: "Supply creates its own demand." Since only by supplying goods or services can anyone ultimately buy anything, it is the supplies, rather than the money, that actually creates the demand. The basis of economics is still barter or trading. Money just hugely increases the efficiency of the process.

As Reagan recognized, money alone, how ever rebated or redistributed by government, does not create demand at all. Republicans should never, ever use the word "stimulus package," which implies that the government can stimulate economic growth by redistributing money. Republicans should never support tax rebates or targeted tax cuts. A targeted tax cut is just another form of government spending, since it assigns so-called government funds to people who do the government's bidding in some way, such as growing corn for ethanol or avoiding marriage.

Under the supply-side regime, the only valuable role of government with regard to money is to maintain a stable currency. What an investor needs is the assurance that he will be repaid or make future payments in money that has not drastically changed in worth. All long-term economic activity depends on a predictable unit of account and transactions. In this role, money is an instrument of memory and measure. It is an accounting device. All that matters is that it keep its value—that governments do not manipulate it and destroy its predictability through alternating regimes of inflation and deflation, strong dollars and weak dollars.

Only the supply of goods or services lends value to money and thus creates purchasing power. Only policies that increase the incentive and ability to produce can do anything to enlarge demand or expand government revenues. That is the key supply-side insight. Supply creates its own demand.

This is the moral heart of Reagan's message. The reason for tax cuts is *not* to allow the rich to keep their money. It is to enable them to invest it by making their investments profitable. Through the investment process, entrepreneurs give money to others either in their own businesses or in other businesses. That is, they pay employees and purchase shares of stock or lend money to other entrepreneurs. Through earning the money they learned how to identify the best people to make it grow. They learned how to use the money in ways that respond to the needs of others, their customers.

High tax rates do not prevent you from keeping your existing wealth. They do not stop you from being rich. If you are already rich, you can move your money to some protected haven. High tax rates stop poor people from getting rich. They stop you from supplying new goods and services that generate more wealth and jobs and value and tax revenues.

Supply creates its own demand. Think of it. There is rarely any demand for new things. Supply creates demand. Risk is always present. Market surveys cannot determine the demand for some product that no one has seen or understands. In my office I have an old photograph of the half-completed Golden Gate bridge in San Francisco. Underneath, it says, "You cannot build a bridge by counting the swimmers." That is, you cannot tell where to build a bridge by looking in the water for people trying to swim across.

Supply-side economics focuses not on the desire for things but on the creation of them, not on the dollars in people's pockets but the ideas in their heads. To defend tax cuts because they allow you to *keep* your money is the opposite of the case. Tax cuts are good because they allow you to give your money to others, in an ever-expanding spiral of economic opportunity. In the end, the rich can keep only what they give away. That is, what they entrust to others in the ever-spreading process of investment and growth.

It pains me to say it, but today, the U.S. is no longer the spearhead of world capitalist growth and supply-side economics—no longer the lead vessel of Ronald Reagan's low tax and deregulatory regime. The global capitalist economy is undergoing an epochal inversion, with Europe and the U.S. sinking into a bureaucratic slough, over-taxed, over-regulated, and technophobic, while the former communist world is giving up its hammer and sickle and picking up the Reagan cleaver and scythe. Usurping the Reagan mantle and capitalist vanguard are the countries of the former Soviet Union, with its 13 percent national flat tax, and the People's Republic of China, with its zero marginal rates on agricultural output, its zero capital gains tax, its engineering dominated educational system, its coastal free zones with their entrepreneurial culture of riotous growth and creativity.

Let me offer a further rule of supply-side economics. Don't solve problems. Solve problems and you end up feeding your failures, starving your strengths, and achieving costly mediocrity. Pursue opportunities. I recently returned from a week in China, my first visit since 1988. I was addressing a *Forbes* CEO conference in Hong Kong, which, under the new model of "one nation, many systems," is now part of China.

Washington tends to see China as a problem. I think it is in fact the greatest opportunity in the history of capitalism. Washington deems former Chairman Jiang Zemin a dangerous communist. I believe that Jiang is the single most inspirational capitalist political leader of the day, comparable to Ronald Reagan. Jiang has adopted the most aggressive supply-side program in the world economy.

Jiang faced the problem that Chinese farmers were not producing their quotas, which constituted a kind of tax on their activities. In such cases, the International Monetary Fund normally recommends increased measures of tax enforcement and collection. Essentially the IMF tells countries that are collecting too little in taxes to raise their rates or prices. Jiang went in the other direction. Any production above the quota, the farmers could keep for themselves or sell for a profit. That meant a zero tax rate on additional production.

To any supply sider aware of the global evidence that lower rates yield higher revenues, the response was predictable. Within three years farm production in China tripled and created the foundations for China's economic miracle. Unleashed by creating free zones in the coastal regions of China, where many farm workers found new employment, the miracle was entirely capitalist. China still supports a huge state-run sector. According to government data, just 514 state-run companies command 59.2 percent of industrial assets and 49.4 percent of profits. But the number of registered private businesses has increased explosively, from 90,000 in 1998 to 2.3 million in 2001. Farms continue to expand food production. The growth and opportunity is emerging from essentially private companies which are now estimated to comprise some 80 percent of Chinese output.

The Chinese economy took off before the Russian economy did because Jiang had the advantage of seeing what had not worked in the Soviet Union. Deregulating from the center, the inside out, the Russians tried to liberate the entire economy at once. This Russian policy aroused maximum resistance by the entrenched, established forces in Russia. China, instead, created free zones where capitalist activity could prosper. Rather than exerting force from the center and evoking resistance across the country, China created local magnetic fields of freedom that attracted people from across the country. In China, everyone outside the free zones wanted to move into them to gain the manifest benefits of freedom.

Jiang's program has evoked growth so explosive as to be unbelievable were it not visible for all to see. The communist Chairman Mao once famously declared, in an effort to flush out his enemies, "Let a thousand flowers bloom." In 1988, shortly before the famous fiasco of Tiannamen Square, I made a visit to Shanghai and called on Chinese leaders to "let a billion flowers bloom." That is what has happened in China. It illustrates as dramatically as any other example the impact of lower tax rates, redistributing not income but tax payers, and multiplying their numbers and payments.

On my trips to Hong Kong, I would always run up over the top of the mountain that overlooks the bay on one side and offers a vista of China on the other. On the other side of the mountain from Hong Kong, I could see the barren reaches of Communist China in the distance. Until the last decade, the town on the Communist side, Shenzhen, was nearly invisible, a cluster of shacks and shanties ghostly through the fog.

A special free-zone project of Chairman Jiang, in the past decade Shenzhen has gone from being a sleepytime Communist town of 40,000 people to a thriving city of 6 million with a towering skyline. It is the scheduled site for a Chinese "NASDAQ" stock exchange oriented toward bringing potential liquidity to high tech venture investments. Within the magnetic field of Shenzhen, but outside the free zone, is Dong Guan to the north, a city full of small businesses and down market manufacturers, that has grown from two million to nine million during this insurgence. Under the influence of the World Trade Organization and its disciplines, China is sloughing off the coils of communism and becoming a world capitalist vanguard.

And yet all this is regarded as a problem in Washington, where the threat to Taiwan is considered particularly menacing. Indeed, Jiang has had to deal with the crippling burden of China's Communist apparatus and Communist army. He has had to confront memories of the Taiwanese humiliation of China, when this little island on the edge of China outproduced the mainland. At the *Forbes* conference, I talked to Morris Chang, who used to be vice president of Texas Instruments and who moved to Taiwan to establish the Taiwan Semiconductor Manufacturing Corporation. It has become the largest and most advanced "foundry" or independent semiconductor fabrication facility in the world. The leading business figure in technology in Taiwan, Chang is investing nearly a billion dollars in silicon wafer fabricators on the mainland. His chief problem is that the United States has restrictions on what size geometries you can transport to China—as if somehow China is a problem, and Chinese prosperity is a threat rather than an immense and thrilling opportunity for the world economy. If Morris Chang is willing to embrace mainland China, Washington should be ready as well.

There is absolutely no possibility that U.S. regulations can stop the advance of Chinese electronics technology. American technology will soon be as dependent on China as Chinese technology will be dependent on the U.S. But U.S. regulation can continue to wreak devastation in the communications and optical technologies in which the U.S. has led the world ever since Reagan made a free zone of the entire U.S. economy. Such challenges, however, are not unusual in U.S. history and the U.S. has thrived in the face of them. Chinese institutions now graduate some ten times as many engineers as we do. But during the sixties and seventies, the Soviet Union also produced three times as many scientists and engineers as we did, and there were many dolorous predictions of the future of the U.S. in the face of the challenge of the Soviet Union. Later came the challenge of Japan and its supposedly impregnable wall of giant corporations in combination with government guidance.

The United States responded with entrepreneurial creativity. We changed the rules of the game and compensated for the educational failures of American students by attracting immigrants to U.S. technical universities. While our own elites studied pettifoggery and environmental phobias, we allowed foreign countries to supply the engineering talent needed by Silicon Valley's entrepreneurs. We changed the field of engagement, and provided a cornucopia of new inventions that erupted in the Internet and the personal computer revolutions. Those two great themes have carried the U.S. economy forward.

Now emerging as the most aggressive capitalist competitors in the world economy are the former Communist countries China and Russia. Russia still seems afflicted with many problems, but as long as it continues the emancipation of its economy and maintain its new 13 percent flat tax, mark my words: Russia will rival China as one of the fastest growing economies in the world.

This is a new kind of challenge for the U.S. Until now, the U.S. has maintained capitalist dominance because of the Marxist myths that hobbled its rivals. Today, the leading source of Marxist myth in the world is the U.S. university. That is why Hillsdale College remains such a precious resource for the United States economy and culture. While the U.S. now faces newly liberated rivals, Hillsdale still benefits from the stultifying regimes of Marxism, technophobia, and triviality that afflict most of its competitors, and all the elite Ivy League schools of the East and West.

To thrive in this new world of the capitalist inversion, the U.S. will have to change the rules of the game again. It must recapture the inspiration of Ronald Reagan on the supply side. It must return to the truths long upheld and celebrated at Hillsdale. It must promote the values that lend value to the production of the land.

This means learning how to educate our own children in math and science, and even in history and supply-side economics. It means unleashing the broadband Internet economy now paralyzed by regulation and litigation. It means recognizing that no tax rates over 20 percent collect any net revenues. It means lowering tax rates to the levels that are imposed by our competitors. It means that George W. Bush has to adopt the supply-side inspiration of Ronald Reagan. I think he has, with the help of a Republican Congress. But he cannot do it alone. He must have the support of the culture, and in the face of the slough of obscurantism in other colleges across the country, Hillsdale can play an absolutely critical role in the future of American education and economics. And as Hillsdale supplies the truth, it will discover once again, that supply creates its own demand.

As Ronald Reagan said in his famous speech to the Moscow students, "Even as we explore the most advanced reaches of science, we are returning to the age-old wisdom of our culture. As we read in Genesis: 'In the beginning was the spirit, and it was from this spirit that the material abundance of creation issued forth.'" This is the ultimate supply-side insight, that wealth springs not from matter or money but from the human mind and spirit.

Notes

[1]Keith Marsden, "Taxes and Growth," in *Finance and Development* (Washington, D.C.: International Monetary Fund and World Bank), September 1983.

[2]Jude Wanniski and David Goldman, with Jay Turner and Evan Kalimtgis, "A Flat Tax Would Produce Explosive U.S. Economic Growth," *Supply-Side Analytics* (Morristown, NJ: Polyconomics, 1992).

[3]Economic Experts Group, "Federal Budget Execution," <www.eeg.iru/(e)budget.html>.

WILLIAM R. DOUGAN

What Is the Chicago School?

Chicago is the quintessential American city: productive, unpretentious, and open. As they describe the city of Chicago, so too do these characteristics define the university that bears its name. Strikingly young by the standards of the world's great schools, the University of Chicago has, in its 110 years of existence, given us big-time college football, the nuclear reactor, and a school of thought that was instrumental in advancing the cause of freedom as much as the quality of economic analysis in the twentieth century.

The Chicago School of Economics is not now, and has never been, merely an alias for the Department of Economics at the University of Chicago. A partial list of the many eminent economists who have been members of the department but who have never been, and would never have wanted to be, associated with the Chicago School as I shall define it must include Thorstein Veblen, Oskar Lange, and Paul Douglas. If one extends the list to include those affiliated with the University as members of the Cowles Commission, which was located at Chicago from 1939 to 1954, then it includes Nobel laureates Kenneth Arrow, Gerard Debreu, Tjalling Koopmans, and Herbert Simon, among others—decidedly not names often, or indeed ever, associated with the Chicago School.

Conversely, there are certain economists who are truly Chicagoans despite never having studied or taught there: Armen Alchian, Ron Jones, Douglass North, and my late colleague Don Gordon come readily to mind, and of course it seems impossible that the great quantity theorist Irving Fisher spent his entire academic career at Yale. An epigram attributed to Paul Samuelson makes this point perfectly: "Chicago is not a place but a state of mind."[1] (It is not clear what state of mind Professor Samuelson associates with Chicago, of course.)

If the Chicago School is not simply a leading economics department, what is it, and why is it worth talking about in this forum?

I will begin with an anecdote. In the fall of my first year in graduate school I attended a meeting of the Libertarian Club of the University of Chicago at which George Stigler was to speak on "The Meaning of Freedom." As you can probably imagine, libertarians at Chicago then were a particularly pure strain of the species, and I myself did not lack a certain ardor in my attachment to that worldview. So you can also probably imagine the stir that Stigler precipitated when he told us that he was simply unable to perceive a meaningful distinction between freedom and wealth. The details of his argument are not important for my purposes today. What *is* important is that, 28 years later, I still find myself thinking about what he said.

Stigler's provocation represented the essence of the Chicago state of mind: Challenge everything, particularly people's most dearly held (and so, in all likelihood, their least critically examined) beliefs. In this way does the Chicago School implement the University's motto: *Crescat scientia, vita excolatur* ("Let knowledge grow, and life enriched.") No true Chicagoan ever says, "How can you *think* that?" in response to a provocative statement. He will, instead, ask, "*Why* do you think that?" If the answer offered in reply does not have a logical and empirical basis, only *then* will it be rejected. This is the ultimate in intellectual freedom, and to generations of economists it has proven exhilarating.

The Defining Features of the Chicago School

Methodology

One of the defining features of a Chicago economist is his adherence to certain methodological precepts. Milton Friedman's lecture notes on price theory[2] served as the introduction to these precepts for a generation of graduate students. The core precepts are:

1. *People and firms are, or act as if they are, rational maximizers of utility or profit.*

The assumption that all individuals and firms are purposeful maximizers is the default assumption in all cases. There is no need for a different economics of the aggregate economy or of poor societies or of large institutions (corporate or bureaucratic, private or public) from the economics we use to study a simple competitive firm.

The *locus classicus* of this view is Friedman's 1953 essay, "The Methodology of Positive Economics,"[3] in which he offers his well-known billiard-player example.

> Consider the problem of predicting the shots made by an expert billiard player. It seems not at all unreasonable that excellent predictions would be yielded by the hypothesis that the billiard player made his shots *as if* he knew the complicated mathematical formulas that would give the optimum directions of travel, could estimate accurately by eye the angles, etc., describing the location of the balls, could make lightning calculations from the formulas, and could then make the balls travel in the direction indicated by the formulas. . . . It is only a short step from these examples to the economic hypothesis that under a wide range of circumstances individual firms behave *as if* they were seeking rationally to maximize their expected returns . . . and had full knowledge of the relevant cost and demand functions. . . .

The critical passage comes two paragraphs later.

> An even more important body of evidence for the maximization-of-returns hypothesis is experience from countless applications of the hypothesis to specific problems and the repeated failure of its implications to be contradicted.

This is the essence of the Chicago worldview. Its working assumption is that people are generally rational, an assumption that will be maintained as long as it generates testable implications that fail to be refuted by empirical evidence.

These arguments now, fifty years after their publication, are the stuff of introductory textbooks.

In an era in which the popular press abounds with references to corporate executives with nicknames like "Chainsaw Al," it is perhaps hard for today's students to believe that at one time corporate managers were criticized, at least implicitly, for their purported *failure* to maximize profits. Instead, viewed as largely unmonitored by their diffuse and indifferent shareholders, these "organization men" were believed to advance the well-being and social status of themselves and their subordinates, subject only to the constraint that they deliver to their owners a "satisfactory" rate of return. The pricing and production decisions of such managers were held by some to be unanalyzable in terms of the standard economic framework. Something new, and most likely something sociological, would be needed to analyze what J. K. Galbraith subsequently termed "the new industrial state." While something as quaint as supply and demand analysis might still be useful in analyzing the price of wheat, it was widely viewed as wholly inadequate to explain the determination of the "administered prices" of the modern industrial sector.

2. Partial-equilibrium analysis is a useful tool of applied economic analysis.

The Chicago School is typically Marshallian, not Walrasian. It holds that, for many if not most applications, the parsimony of partial-equilibrium analysis renders it more useful than general-equilibrium methods. Even Arnold Harberger's general-equilibrium approach to the measurement of allocative inefficiency[4] has been ingeniously designed to be explicable in a simple Marshallian framework.

This feature is perhaps the most enduring source of disagreement among the economists at Chicago, as distinct from the Chicago School. The research on general-equilibrium theory conducted by economists on the staff of the Cowles Commission during its affiliation with Chicago would ultimately garner several Nobel prizes, but the departure of that group for Yale in 1955 can be viewed in part as a resolution of the tension between practitioners of partial and general-equilibrium methods. Such differences are perhaps increasingly a matter of degree rather than of stark contrast, especially in the realm of macroeconomic modeling. It remains the case, however, that one of the surest ways to identify a Chicago Schooler is his admiration for the simple clarity of the concepts of supply and demand curves.

3. *Useful economic theories generate testable hypotheses.*

The importance of economics lies in its ability to explain human behavior. The ultimate test of that ability is the conformity of analytical conclusions with empirical observation. The Chicago School shares Koopmans's famous rejection of "measurement without theory."[5] However, it also disdains theory without measurement, by which I mean analytical exercises that generate implications that are inherently incapable of being refuted by empirical observation.

Gary Becker, reflecting on his introduction to the Chicago approach in the first-year price theory class, observed:

> Friedman emphasized that economic theory was not a game played by clever academicians, but was a powerful tool to analyze the real world. His course was filled with insights both into the structure of economic theory and its application to practical and significant questions.[6]

Worldview

By "worldview" I mean that set of beliefs about the nature of society that adherents of the Chicago School tend to share. It is the set of hypotheses that are consistent with both the methodological precepts listed above and the available empirical evidence. The essential aspects of the Chicago worldview are:

1. *Individual markets tend toward equilibrium.*

This does *not* necessarily imply that markets *are* in equilibrium at any particular moment, although it is certainly the case that a theory that specifies the precise impediments to the attainment of equilibrium is certainly preferable to one that does not. What this proposition *does* imply is that the concept of equilibrium is not merely useful, but indispensable, for figuring out where a particular market is heading over the relevant period of time. It most definitely constitutes a rejection of the notion that the path of development of a market or an economy is utterly unknowable and therefore unpredictable.

In the words of Arnold Harberger:

> ... our vision—certainly my own vision, which I believe is shared by nearly all or all of my colleagues at Chicago—is that the forces of the market are just that: They are forces; they are like the wind and the tides; they are things that if you want to try to ignore them, you ignore them at your peril. . . .[7]

There are innumerable examples of this principle being applied to the analysis of market performance. I will cite but one, the famous essay by Milton Friedman and George Stigler, *Roofs or Ceilings?*[8]

In their essay, Friedman and Stigler contrast the response of the San Francisco housing market in the aftermath of the 1906 earthquake, in which a city of about 400,000 people lost about half its housing stock in a three-day period, to the same market's performance under rent control in 1946. The essential premise of this clear and persuasive essay is that, left to its own operation, the housing market in San Francisco, and presumably elsewhere, will tend remarkably quickly to an equilibrium set of prices in which the quantities offered for purchase and those sought are brought into equality.

Friedman and Stigler then proceed to contrast the outcomes resulting from rationing by price with those that tend to prevail under nonprice rationing, and argue persuasively that the allocation of housing resources resulting from the operation of a free market is superior to the allocations resulting from other rationing methods. The particular market under analysis is unique in terms of time and location, but it is abundantly clear that the lessons to be learned from this essay generalize quite readily to most other markets.

2. *Markets in the aggregate tend toward equilibrium at full employment of all resources.*

The investigation of this proposition was the principal theoretical and empirical undertaking of twentieth-century economics, and it was a centerpiece of economic research and writing at Chicago from the era of Jacob Viner and Henry Simons to the development of the rational-expectations paradigm in macroeconomics. To reduce a long, detailed, and at times passionate research agenda to a single word, Chicago's answer to the question *Is capitalism stable?* is, "Yes."

This is, of course, a complete rejection of what was once called the Keynesian Revolution. It is a proposition that leads directly to a rejection of such key elements of the Keynesian model as a stable trade-off between wage or price inflation and the economywide rate of unemployment. Subsequent work by Robert Lucas on rational expectations articulated the Chicago critique of Keynesian models of the aggregate economy in detail.[9]

It is the presumption of full employment as the normal state of an economy that gives microeconomic analysis its relevance. In a world of chronic underemployment, the problems imposed by scarcity would be irrelevant. The overriding issue would be how best to attain and sustain full employment.

3. Unhindered market processes tend to allocate resources efficiently.

The overwhelming number of markets in an economy are explained well by the model of perfect competition. The Fundamental Theorem of Welfare Economics tells us that, aside from some potential complications arising from spillover effects and public goods, an unregulated economy provides the most reliable route to individual well-being *as defined by individuals themselves.*

Research by Chicagoans in the related fields of industrial organization and law and economics has provided much of the logical and empirical support for this view of the efficiency of laissez-faire. George Stigler, Lester Telser, Harold Demsetz, and Sam Peltzman, among others, challenged the view that large firms and concentrated industries were necessarily anticompetitive. Furthermore, they argued persuasively that regulation of industries is more likely to maintain noncompetitive prices through entry restrictions than to serve the interests of consumers.

The most fundamental contribution to this essential Chicago viewpoint was, of course, made by Ronald Coase. His penetrating analysis of the reciprocal nature of spillover effects, and the incentives for bargaining that arise as a natural consequence of those spillovers, revolutionized the economic analysis of externalities.[10]

For these reasons, the essential policy conclusion of the Chicago School is that distortions of competitive equilibrium, usually resulting from ill-conceived government policies, are the likeliest impediments to individual well-being in most situations. Policies that ignore or run counter to ordinary people's efforts to better their lives and their children's lives are certain to do more harm than good. Evidence in support of this view has been accumulated from a wide variety of experiences. The work of Theodore W. Schultz on agriculture and economic development is notable for its breadth, its carefulness, and its clarity. In his Nobel lecture Schultz observed:

> Although farmers differ for reasons of schooling, health and experience in their ability to perceive, to interpret and to take appropriate action in responding to new information, they provide an essential human resource which is entrepreneurship. . . . Where governments have taken over this function in farming, they have prevented this entrepreneurial talent from being used and these governments have been unsuccessful in providing an effective allocative substitute, capable of modernizing agriculture.[11]

4. *The principal source of nominal instability throughout history has been fluctuation in the stock of money.*

A corollary of this is Friedman's famous observation that "Sustained inflation is always and everywhere a monetary phenomenon." The empirical foundation for this view was established principally by Milton Friedman and Anna Schwartz in their *Monetary History of the United States.*[12] The many Chicago dissertations analyzing the experiences of other countries, particularly during periods of extremely high inflation, contributed brick after brick to the monetarist edifice.

5. *Economics is imperial in its relations with other social sciences, and properly so.*

The wide-ranging and insightful work by Gary Becker and his students, on subjects ranging from racial discrimination to the criminal

justice system to the management of the household (from which economics derives its name), has pushed the boundaries of economics
deep into the territories formerly claimed by sociology, psychology,
and political science. The colonization of political science by economists, of course, was pioneered by James Buchanan and Gordon Tullock, both Chicago products—Buchanan a protege of Frank Knight
and Tullock a pupil of Henry Simons. While it is customary to distinguish between the Chicago and Virginia schools of thought in political economy, the latter is undeniably Chicago-like in its efforts to
extend the reach of economics beyond its traditional borders. The
principal difference between these two schools of thought seems to
arise largely from the Virginians' markedly greater level of interaction with the indigenous peoples of political science and philosophy.

The Successes of the Chicago School

Money and Prices

No economists argue seriously that monetary policy exerts no effect
on the economy; now it is the efficacy of fiscal policy that is in doubt.
This represents a complete reversal of the standard views of the professional economists in the 1950s and 1960s.

One day recently while surfing the Internet I happened upon
the website of one Steve Kangas, a self-described liberal (in the contemporary sense), where the following statement was posted:

> . . . virtually all economists agree that the total amount or value
> of money in a system should closely match its level of economic
> activity. If there is too much money, then inflation rises.[13]

It is, of course, possible to quibble with the precise wording of this
statement, but its intended meaning seems clear; its author is essentially a monetarist. What is striking about this statement is not its content, but its source. When simple monetarist propositions are taken
for granted by ordinary people who consider themselves to be on the
left politically, a sea change in perceptions has occurred. For those of
you too young to know to remember, let me assure you that the propo-

sition advanced in the preceding quote was emphatically *not* ascribed to by "virtually all economists" in the 1960s. Theories with such names as "administered prices," "cost-push inflation," and "functional finance" were widely viewed as respectable, indeed mainstream, explanations for the rise (no other direction of price movement was even contemplated) of the general level of prices. Friedman's contention that "sustained inflation is always and everywhere a monetary phenomenon" caused him to be derided as a crank by the self-styled mainstream thinkers of the postwar era.

Prices and Output

Although this is a much less settled area, it is nevertheless an issue on which the Chicago School has influenced both economists and policymakers of all stripes. Since Friedman's presidential address to the American Economic Association in 1967,[14] the idea that there is an exploitable long-run trade-off between unemployment and inflation has ceased to represent mainstream opinion. In its place stands a general consensus that the principal responsibility of the Federal Reserve System is to stabilize the general level of prices. Although this change in thinking is probably attributable in large measure to the clear monetary policy failures of the 1970s, the theoretical innovation that helped explain the reason for those policy failures was the crucial distinction between anticipated and unanticipated events and their disparate effects on the actions of rational maximizers of utility or profits.[15]

Economic Development

The 1970s were the heyday of completely hedged Nobel prize awards in economics. The first of these was the joint award to Friedrich Hayek and Gunnar Myrdal in 1974, followed five years later by the pairing of Theodore Schultz with Sir Arthur Lewis. Recall Schultz's view that the best thing for government to do in developing countries is to stop distorting the prices faced by entrepreneurial farmers, and contrast it with Lewis's belief that entrepreneurship may falter, in which case,

Much of the responsibility for maintaining momentum then falls on the government, given its large share of the cash economy, and also the extent to which it regulates or supports the private sector.[16]

The next two decades brought stark and dramatic evidence of the vitality of private entrepreneurs and the stultifying effects of heavy government involvement in the economies of the noncapitalist countries. The eventual ascendancy of Schultz's view of the development process, and its practical implementation by generations of students taught by him and Arnold Harberger and D. Gale Johnson, has been most clearly demonstrated by the superb PBS documentary *Commanding Heights* [based on the book by Daniel Yergin and Joseph Stanislaw]. I can assure you that, as surprising as it seems today that so insightful a program would be broadcast on public television, in 1979 it was utterly unimaginable.

Government Regulation and Taxation

The Chicago influence here has been so extensive that I can merely offer a quick survey of its key impacts on public policy. A short list includes these obvious examples:

1. The importance of marginal tax rates on the incentives to work, save, and invest are widely recognized. Evidence of this is the decline in the top marginal income-tax rate to 38.6 percent today, from 91 percent in 1963.
2. The relative efficacy of free entry of new firms compared to government regulation of existing firms is a generally accepted principle. As a consequence of this new view, airlines, banks, and communications (just to go through the abc's) have all been deregulated.
3. Antitrust policy is no longer predicated on the axiom that "big is bad." It is much more receptive to the possibility that firms become big because they are efficient.
4. Market-based approaches to environmental policy are now an accepted part of the regulatory arsenal. Even the Kyoto treaty calls for tradeable pollution rights.

Conclusion

The fundamental contribution of the Chicago School has been its ability to demonstrate *to those not predisposed to agree with it* that prosperity and individual liberty go hand in hand. Though it is nearly a truism today, this proposition was by no means obvious in 1933 or even in 1963. The intellectual successes of the Chicago School are attributable directly to its commitment to the development of falsifiable hypotheses from a simple theory of human behavior and to the careful empirical testing of those hypotheses. Whatever differences may exist among the various conservative schools of economic thought, all of them would have been marginalized without the efforts of the Chicago School and its direct engagement with mainstream economic thought.

In closing, let me quote from what can be considered the manifesto of the Chicago School, *Capitalism and Freedom,* on the challenge facing economists who share Milton Friedman's views on liberty:

> The basic problem of social organization is how to co-ordinate the economic activities of large numbers of people. Even in relatively backward societies, extensive division of labor and specialization of function is required to make effective use of available resources. In advanced societies, the scale on which coordination is needed, to take full advantage of the opportunities offered by modern science and technology, is enormously greater. Literally millions of people are involved in providing one another with their daily bread, let alone with their yearly automobiles. *The challenge to the believer in liberty is to reconcile this widespread interdependence with individual freedom.* [emphasis added]

What, then, is the Chicago School? In brief, I would argue that it is the group of researchers and teachers whose careers have ultimately served to meet the challenge laid down by Friedman. Their combination of simple economic logic and relentless empirical testing has proven to be the most effective approach to advancing the cause of liberty by expanding our understanding of the market form of social organization and its alternatives.

Notes

[1] Quoted in Allen R. Sanderson, "Wealth of Notions," *University of Chicago Alumni Magazine* (December 2001).

[2] Milton Friedman, *Price Theory* (New York, NY: Aldine de Gruyter, 1976).

[3] Milton Friedman, *Essays in Positive Economics* (Chicago, IL: University of Chicago Press, 1953).

[4] Arnold C. Harberger, "Three Basic Postulates for Applied Welfare Economics: An Interpretive Essay," *Journal of Economic Literature* 9 (September 1971): 785–97.

[5] Tjalling C. Koopmans, "Measurement without Theory," *Review of Economics and Statistics* 29 (August 1947): 161–72.

[6] Gary S. Becker, "Autobiography," at <http://www.nobel.se/economics/laureates/1992/becker-autobio.html>.

[7] From transcript of interview for *Commanding Heights*, at http://www.pbs.org/wgbh/commandingheights/shared/minitextlo/int_alharberger.html

[8] Milton Friedman and George J. Stigler, *Roofs or Ceilings? The Current Housing Problem* (Irvington-on-Hudson, NY: Foundation for Economic Education, 1946).

[9] Robert E. Lucas, Jr., "Econometric Policy Evaluation: A Critique." In *The Phillips Curve and Labor Markets*, K. Brunner and A. Meltzer, eds. *Carnegie-Rochester Conference Series on Public Policy* (Amsterdam: North-Holland, 1976).

[10] Ronald H. Coase, "The Problem of Social Cost," *Journal of Law & Economics* 3 (October 1960): 1–44.

[11] Theodore W. Schultz, "Nobel Lecture: The Economics of Being Poor," *Journal of Political Economy* 88 (August 1980): 639–51.

[12] Milton Friedman and Anna J. Schwartz, *A Monetary History of the United States, 1867–1960.* (Princeton, NJ: Princeton University Press for the National Bureau of Economic Research, 1963).

[13] See <http://www.huppi.com/kangaroo/L-ausgold.htm>.

[14] Milton Friedman, "The Role of Monetary Policy," *American Economic Review* 58 (March 1968): 1–17.

[15] Robert E. Lucas, Jr., "Nobel Lecture: Monetary Neutrality," *Journal of Political Economy* 104 (August 1996): 661–82.

[16] W. Arthur Lewis, "The Slowing Down of the Engine of Growth," *American Economic Review* 70 (September 1980): 555–64.

[17] Milton Friedman, *Capitalism and Freedom* (University of Chicago Press, 1962), pp. 12–13.

NOLAN FINLEY

Free Markets: Future Controversies

This little fable came to my attention under the heading "The Truth About Taxes." It truly is that.

It puts tax cuts in terms everyone can understand. Suppose that every day, ten men go out for dinner. The bill for all ten comes to $100. If they paid their bill the way we pay our taxes, it would go something like this:

> The first four men, the poorest, would pay nothing; the fifth would pay $1, the sixth would pay $3; the seventh $7; the eighth $12; the ninth $18. The tenth man—the richest—would pay $59. That is what they decided to do.
>
> The ten men ate dinner in the restaurant every day and seemed quite happy with the arrangement—until one day, the owner threw them a curve. "Since you are all such good customers," he said, "I'm going to reduce the cost of your daily meal by $20." So now dinner for the ten only cost $80. The group still wanted to pay the bill the way we pay our taxes. So the first four men were unaffected. They would still eat for free. But what about the other six—the paying customers?
>
> How could they divvy up the $20 windfall so that everyone would get his "fair share?" The six men realized that $20 divided by six is $3.33. But if they subtracted that from everybody's share, then the fifth man and the sixth man would end up being "paid" to eat their meal. So the restaurant owner suggested that it would be fair to reduce each man's bill proportionately, and he

proceeded to work out the amounts each should pay. And so the fifth man now paid nothing, the sixth pitched in $2, the seventh paid $5, the eighth paid $9, the ninth paid $12, leaving the tenth man with a bill of $52 instead of his earlier $59. Everyone was happy at first. Each of the six was better off than before. And the first four continued to eat for free. But once outside the restaurant, the men began to compare their savings.

"I only got a dollar out of the $20," declared the sixth man. He pointed to the tenth. "But he got $7!" "Yeah, that's right," exclaimed the fifth man. "I only saved a dollar, too. It's unfair that he got seven times more than me!" "That's true!" shouted the seventh man. "Why should he get $7 back when I got only $2? The wealthy get all the breaks!"

"Wait a minute," yelled the first four men in unison. "We didn't get anything at all. The system exploits the poor!" The nine men surrounded the tenth and beat him up. The next night he didn't show up for dinner, so the nine sat down and ate without him. But when it came time to pay the bill, they discovered something important. They were $52 short!

And that is exactly how the tax system works. The people who pay the highest taxes get the most benefit from a tax reduction. Tax them too much, attack them for being wealthy, and they just may not show up at the table anymore.

That little story goes right to the heart of the current debate over how to reform the tax code and provide tax relief to the people who actually pay taxes, so that they can invest in the economy and create jobs for everyone else.

I am not an economist. I also have very little in common with Nostradamus: I have no crystal ball. I am simply a commentator, someone who gets paid to offer his opinion on this, that, and the other thing. With that disclaimer, I will give you my thoughts on what I see as some of the greatest challenges facing America's free market system in coming years. There are many—as there always have been.

Modern capitalism, which has its roots in sixteenth-century English commerce, has allowed Western culture to flourish, to become the most prosperous, the most dominant, the most free culture ever to grace the face of the earth. It has proven its merits over and over again. Yet, as much as we have benefited from free and open markets, as fervently as we preach to other nations the effectiveness of unfettered commerce in improving a society's quality of life, we cannot resist tinkering.

We still aren't entirely convinced that the marketplace is the most honest regulator. We want to add a little more weight to one side of the scale or the other, to make things more balanced, more fair. Witness George W. Bush's completely unwarranted lapse into protectionism last year when he slapped tariffs on steel imports. That decision, driven by principles of politics rather than economics, is paying off just as many predicted.

Yes, the steel companies are enjoying stronger revenues—for the short-term. But their customers, particularly in the automotive industry, are reeling. They are laying off workers. They may have to shut plants, or move them overseas. They are far less able to compete in an extremely brutal marketplace than they were when they were free to buy the best steel at the best price.

Ultimately, the cost of just about everything made of steel will be higher for consumers, and the overall market for steel makers will shrink. This should be tattooed on our brains: Tariffs and trade barriers are bad for the economy. Toss them out, tear them down, and you create jobs and more wealth for both trading partners.

At this country's founding, Ben Franklin reminded his peers that "no nation was ever ruined by trade." George W. Bush knows this as well as you and I do, if not better. Yet when it came to the steel tariffs, he placed political expediency ahead of sound economic principles. That is what politicians do.

That is another important fact to remember as we consider the current Big Daddy of all challenges facing the free market system. It is not protectionism, at least not right now. We have always had to fight protectionist urges, and we likely always will.

Where we risk taking a giant step toward controlled markets, toward socialism if you will, is through the door of health care. America's competitive, profit-driven health care system has produced the very best medicines, the top physicians, and the finest hospitals.

Not only do we have the best quality health care, we also have the most accessible health care. In this country, we don't have to wait in long lines outside clinics, or sign up weeks in advance to see a physician like they do in nations with national health care systems.

In Canada, during a severe outbreak of influenza, it can take up to six weeks to get a doctor's appointment. By the time six weeks have passed, you are either going to be better, or you are going to be buried. We don't face that in America, nor do we face the rationing of health services as patients do in Europe. A competitive health care market has fairly well matched supply of services to demand for services.

A profit-driven system also continues to drive medical innovations and inventions. American researchers produce drugs, techniques, and procedures that save lives today, and add years to life expectancy. But it ain't cheap. In fact, the cost is stunning. Spending on health care stands at about $1.5 trillion dollars a year, and is predicted to rise at 10 percent or more annually for the foreseeable future. For employers who offer a health insurance benefit, premiums climbed an average of 12 percent last year. That is a huge bite out of profits.

Government-sponsored insurance programs, Medicaid and Medicare, are rising at 8 to 11 percent a year. In Michigan, spending on Medicaid, the health insurance program for the poor, consumes about 19 percent of the state budget, and will grow to 25 percent within five years.

And while we are in Michigan, let's look again at the automobile industry. The three domestic automakers spent $8.2 billion on health care last year for 2.1 million workers, retirees, and dependents. That was up $1 billion, or 13.9 percent, from the year before.

How does that translate to the sticker on the window? About $1,300 of every car sold goes to cover the automakers' health care costs. That helps explain why automotive profits have all but disappeared, despite near record sales volumes.

This obviously can't go on. Decades ago American businesses assumed responsibility for maintaining the health of their employees. Now they are drowning under that commitment. They are desperate for relief.

That relief will come either through a free market solution or from a government solution. A free market solution is the best path, of course, but to get there, we have to shift dramatically the way we think about medicine and medical treatment.

A primary reason for the current crisis in health care affordability is that the consumer of health care is insulated from the cost of health care. About 90 percent of Americans are covered by some sort of private or government health insurance plan. These insurance plans cover most, if not all, of their medical bills.

Most people who go to a clinic for tests, or to a hospital for surgery or for some other medical procedure, never see a bill for those services. Beyond some small deductible they might be required to pay out of their own pockets, they have no clue of the total cost of their treatment.

Dr. Robert Cihak, president of the Association of American Physicians and Surgeons, explains why this isolation of the consumers of health care from the price of health care is a such a major contributor to soaring costs:

> In a normal market, people make quality trade-offs, sometimes substituting less quality for lower costs or greater convenience. However, when people are insulated from the cost of health care because (a third party) is paying the bill, the role of value declines. Patients want quality at any price—because someone else is paying that price. Ironically, when someone else is paying the bill, the insistence upon quality declines because patients are willing to tolerate bad outcomes and poorer services when they are free.[1]

This is basic human nature. We overconsume that which is free. We had a labor strike at my newspaper a few years back, and for a time we were locked in the building. A catering firm was brought in to provide food for the staffers inside. The food wasn't particularly good, but it was free. But after three weeks, we had to kill the food service. Why? Because the 200 people inside the building had eaten enough food to feed 500 people for the same length of time. You looked around the room and people were expanding before your very eyes. Some were eating six meals a day. We had to hold an emergency Weight Watchers seminar. As long as the food was free, there was nothing to check appetites.

Dr. Cihak and other proponents of private medicine advocate a system that forces consumers to become more involved in managing their health care, to share in both the costs and the decisionmaking.

Many employers are beginning to move to insurance plans that ask employees to choose from a menu of benefit options, rather than offering blanket, all-expense-paid coverage, These plans set spending limits and require the patient to cover a greater share of the cost for many procedures. Employees who have to reach into their own wallets to pay a significant portion of health care costs are more likely to ask questions about the value and necessity of the treatment, as well as to consider price when choosing a doctor or hospital.

Hospitals are big advertisers today, but when was the last time you heard a hospital market its value—"we offer the best care at the best price?" They don't have to push that message because that is not how patients choose providers. But it should be part of the decision. When patients are asked to consider the cost of services before they allow their doctors to order them, it not only reduces the demand for health care, it introduces a significant measure of accountability into the system. The patients cannot afford to ignore their hospital bills when they arrive in the mail. They will be more vigilant in reporting suspected fraud. They will challenge their doctors to fully explain why a test is being ordered. They will be informed and savvy consumers. But this is not a popular option with a population that is used to receiving everything, and paying for nothing.

When General Electric asked its workers to cover $300 to $400 a year of their health insurance premiums, it sparked a two-day strike last fall. Many workers on the picket line lost more in wages during those two days than the company was asking them to contribute to their health care. But they were fighting for the principle that health care should be free.

We have enjoyed such broad and low-cost insurance coverage for so long that we have stopped factoring health care as part of the cost of living. We are perfectly willing to pay $100 a month for a cell phone. We'll pay $70 a month for cable television. And we will spend $50 a month for an Internet connection. These are all expenses that did not exist 25 years ago. But please, don't ask us to write out a $100 check for a doctor's visit every couple of months, or to pay $80 for a bottle of heart pills. Some seniors even expect their Viagra to be covered by insurance.

Gaining widespread acceptance for health care reforms that ask individuals to take more financial responsibility will not be easy.

The Big Three automakers will enter into negotiations with their union workers this fall. Given the profit hit the manufacturers are taking from rising health care costs, you would expect that to be *the* primary issue on the table. The automakers have promised Wall Street that they will address health care in this round of talks But don't be surprised if it doesn't happen. The United Auto Workers has made it clear that health care is a nonstarter. They won't talk about it. But if they ever do, it will come at a price. For any concessions the workers make, they will demand in return that the companies throw their weight behind a national health care plan.

That won't take much arm-twisting. It will be much easier for the automakers to off-load their health care costs onto the government than to engage their unions in meaningful reform efforts. The automakers will be joined by the steel industry and other large manufacturing sectors that are saddled with labor contracts that promise more in benefits than the companies can now afford to deliver.

So it will be corporate America—not the unions or the health care advocacy groups—that will lead the charge toward nationalized, or socialized, medicine. Backers of a single-payer system contend it will reduce costs because it will remove the profit from health care and allow that money to be applied to expanding services. Of course, we know that in industry, without competition and without the hope for profits, there is no incentive to contain costs, to satisfy customers, or to deliver quality.

Health care makes up about 14 percent of America's gross domestic product. Ten percent of the national labor force is employed in the health care industry. That is a tremendously large chunk of the economy to remove from the private sector.

If the government takes over, decisionmaking on health care will become more about political expediency and less about maintaining health. Once health care decisions enter the political arena, they will be fair game for partisan wrangling. Politicians, not doctors and patients, will decide who gets health care, how much health care they get, and when and where it will be available.

Does that really sound like a recipe for better health? It will be a disaster, and ultimately it will cost lives. We have to remain committed to solving the health care affordability crisis in this country within the parameters of a free market. That is the only way to assure broad access to top-quality health care, and to preserve the entrepreneurial environment that has led to countless life-saving medical breakthroughs.

U.S. drug companies spend billions of dollars to develop new medicines. To create a drug like Lipitor, for example, thousands of substances are tested over several years. Once a compound is identified as potentially beneficial, the drug manufacturer must submit to prolonged and rigorous government testing for the product to be approved for market.

This system is fertile for the discovery of new miracle medicines because at the end of the road there is the prospect of a double benefit: help for those who are sick, and a profit. If there is a profit, a large portion of it is plowed back into more research to develop the next generation of medicine. This is why free market nations lead the world in creating more effective treatments for ailments ranging from acne to AIDS.

But there is now a sizeable movement for greater federal control over prescription drugs. The critics concentrate on bringing down the price. But if government steps in and regulates price, it will reduce incentive. Less incentive will translate into fewer initiatives to find more effective medicines. Then, of course, that will bring a call for more government spending to do the research now handled by private companies. Given the long record of public waste and mismanagement, there is nothing to indicate that the federal government is capable of such a responsibility, even if it were to take it on.

From health care, let's move to the oldest enemy of free markets—taxation.

I do not have a deep-rooted philosophical objection to paying taxes. I don't like to pay as much in taxes as I do, but I understand that government plays a necessary role in our society and that it has to be funded by the people it serves. But what we have today is a tax code that penalizes success, discourages investment and savings, and robs the free market economy of the capital it needs to expand. The tax code is used as an equalizer to narrow the gap between the lifestyles of those in high-income brackets and those in low-income brackets. This should not be the purpose of taxes.

Efforts to streamline the tax code, making it less progressive and simpler to understand, have been defeated by the politics of class warfare. It seems like ancient history now, but back in 1986, Ronald Reagan achieved a historic tax reform that flattened the tax code to merely two tax brackets—15 and 28 percent. There were some problems with this approach, the biggest being that it increased the cost of capital gains. But otherwise, the Reagan tax reform somewhat simplified the system.

Unfortunately, it didn't last long. No sooner was Reagan out of office than the drums began beating to repeal the reform. It was portrayed as further evidence that the so-called decade of greed had further enriched the rich at the expense of everyone else. The result was that President George Bush the First caved in and committed one of presidential history's greatest blunders. In 1990 he agreed to add more tax brackets as part of a balanced budget agreement. These brackets increased some rates, including a top rate of 38 percent on the highest income.

Clinton further improved things, from the point of view of those who subscribe to the idea that wealth should be more equally distributed. He raised the top tax rate again, and then added new twists to the class envy game. He offered tax breaks—but not across-the-board. Instead, you could receive a child-care tax credit—as long as you didn't make too much money. You could get a break on college expenses—if your family didn't earn too much. Nearly every tax break, including the one you can receive for contributing to an individual retirement account, are now premised on not making "too much money." God forbid that anyone dare make too much.

At the same time, a new definition of "rich" emerged. I will swear on the Bible right here and now that I am not "rich." I live a fairly modest lifestyle. But the government considers me wealthy, and that apparently ticks the government off, because it exempts me from just about every tax break aimed at helping the middle class, or my favorite description, "working families." Just because your family gets up and goes to work every day doesn't make yours a working family in the eyes of the government.

Our politicians will toss you into the wealthy category if your household makes in excess of $80,000 a year. That's a fair income, but it won't buy a yacht in the Greek Isles. A pair of married school teachers can top that mark easily, even though that couple might find it difficult to pay the bills some months, especially if they have a kid in college. Uncle Sam, however, treats them as if they have hit the lottery.

The dirty truth is that class warfare results in a direct attack on the middle class. As more Americans move from the lower middle class and into better jobs, politicians try to find more ways to tap into their wallets and pocketbooks. The middle class is where the money is, after all, and where the government goes to get it. It has had to expand the definition of wealthy to make it easier to milk the middle class. The result is a complex tax code that only the truly wealthy and their lawyers can navigate. In 1939, the tax code was contained on 504 pages. Today, it stands at 46,900. That's nearly 47,000 pages on how to make your money a collective asset.

The current President Bush seems genuinely committed to changing that. Unfortunately, he also seems willing to compromise on some of the fundamental principles of reform. Rather than proportionate relief, he has been inclined to agree to welfare programs cloaked as tax relief—sending tax rebate checks to people who don't pay taxes.

Each tax reform proposal sent to Congress has excused millions more individuals from the tax rolls. Currently, more than 40 percent of working Americans pay no federal income tax. This is creating a two-class system in America where government is funded by one set of earners and functions to serve primarily the other set. It is also shrinking the constituency for true tax reform. If you don't pay taxes, why should you care if the system is oppressive? And why would you volunteer to rejoin the taxpaying ranks?

These so-called reform measures do little to fuel the markets. They are simple wealth transfer schemes whose only benefit is in depriving the federal government of at least some small amount of revenue it would otherwise spend.

But an even more detrimental impact on capitalism is the de-monization of wealth. The desire for wealth, the opportunity to climb the economic ladder through hard work, ambition, skill, intelligence, and luck, has always been part of the American dream. It has inspired our greatest inventions and it has lifted every one of us to a higher standard of living. Take away that opportunity to strike it rich, turn the pursuit of wealth into a negative ambition, and you bring capitalism to a grinding halt.

Along with a tax code that rewards risk and investment, free markets also depend on a rational legal system, and one that is respected by the people it is designed to protect.

Risking money on a capitalistic venture in a place where the law is not consistent and not based on common sense would be foolish. Capitalism needs the legal system to enforce contracts and allow people to seek redress from those who have cheated or lied to them. But the legal system also poses a risk to capitalism. In recent years we have seen a new form of policymaking by litigation. Such efforts reached their zenith with the tobacco lawsuits.

No one argues that tobacco is a hideous product. Use it in any fashion and you increase your risk of serious illness and death. Your mother told you that when you were a child. You learned it again in health class. You probably read the warnings on the back of every cigarette pack. Yet the marketing of tobacco products to adults is and always has been a legal activity. Neither Congress nor any state legislature have mustered the political will to ban tobacco use.

But what lawmakers couldn't do, trial lawyers and state attorneys general could, by using the courts to extract multibillion dollar payoffs from legal companies making legal products, used in exactly the way they were intended. Nobody much objected. Because, after all, cigarettes are bad. Even if the users of tobacco knew the dangers, even if they had been fairly warned of the risks, smoking is nasty, and if the courts could be employed to stop it, why get tangled up in principle?

But the theory behind the tobacco lawsuits ends the presumption that adults can be expected to knowingly assume risks. For most of the history of Anglo-American law, legal liability had to bear a relation to fault. Now that relationship, through mass tort actions, is being severed.

As might have been predicted, it didn't end with tobacco. From there, the trial lawyers moved onto the gun industry—another product short on sympathy—and once again, not for making defective products, but because some individual users of those products have used them in an illegal or improper way.

In Michigan, we have seen the bankruptcy of Dow Corning, a manufacturer of silicone. It was driven into insolvency through mass claims of injury from silicone breast implants—even though the best medical evidence from extensive studies by medical schools at the University of Michigan, Harvard, and many others showed no basis for the claims.

Also driven into bankruptcy was Federal-Mogul, targeted for making asbestos brake liners. Other manufacturers are headed in the same direction, and the Big Three automakers may ultimately have their pockets drained, too. In the case of asbestos, awards are being made to individuals in many instances solely on the basis of exposure, not because they are demonstrating any ill effects from that exposure.

These lawsuits are certainly enriching some individuals and a good number of trial lawyers. But they are killing major corporations, and the jobs they provide.

We are also seeing how the tort system is driving doctors out of practice in states with jurors who award damages like they were passing out pirate's treasure. In protest, doctors have gone on strike in West Virginia. Threatened strikes have led to emergency legislative action in Mississippi and possible action in Pennsylvania. There certainly is medical malpractice and the courts are an appropriate place to seek remedy—but increasingly the legal system seems unable to distinguish bad medical practice from junk science.

Now trial lawyers may even doom the Big Mac. Fast food restaurants are in the sights for selling fattening food that tastes great. These foods, if overconsumed, will make you obese, no doubt about that. But is that your fault or McDonalds'? The good news is that the fast food lawsuits may finally doom frivolous class action suits. The public may tolerate assaults on tobacco, guns, and rich doctors, but tell them they can't supersize their lunch, and you are treading on thin ice.

Ideally, the cure for a runaway tort system lies within the legal system itself. When that doesn't happen, it is up to the state legislatures to provide a fix. In Michigan, very controversial medical malpractice and product liability limitations enacted in the last decade have inspired a torrent of angry rhetoric and huge amounts of campaign donations from the plaintiffs' bar. But the reforms have worked, although they may have to be applied more extensively to keep the courts from snuffing out capitalism.

Who will be willing to invest the time, money, and effort to bring a new product to market knowing the scales of justice are tipped so far against producers? Who will take the risk, when there is the very real possibility that some yahoo will take the product and try to stuff it in his ear, or into some one else's ear, and then sue for damages?

We have to restore common sense and the concept of personal responsibility to the justice system.

Free markets also require reliable avenues of commerce. The future of capitalism hinges in part on nuts-and-bolts issues such as roads and air transport. Commerce demands a physical infrastructure, and our infrastructure is crumbling. In Detroit, businessmen and the Chamber of Commerce are leading the clamor for workable mass transit in a metropolitan area that has none. The business angle is that workers need reliable transportation to reach distant job opportunities, and employers need the transit system to deliver their workers.

The bare bones start on mass transit in Detroit, if adopted, will cost $2 billion. And that is just for a super bus system, not light rail or other more expensive options.

The airline industry, certainly vital to commerce, is on the verge of collapse. Airlines have become the country's de facto system of long-haul mass transit. How they fare will affect the entire economy. But can the airlines continue to operate as private enterprises, or will they require even more government subsidies, perhaps even government takeovers? How many major airlines can the nation afford to lose and still maintain a viable air transportation system?

Given the extraordinary impact of September 11, should the free market be unleashed to work its will on air transit? Should airlines be allowed to succeed or fail on their own ability to compete for customers? Or should there be a tax-supported backstop?

More federal help, of course, invites more federal control. And by definition, more government control over a market makes that market less free and less responsive to customers.

Internationally, the September 11 incident raised security concerns and disputes on solving them. Since 9/11, for example, the United States has struck agreements with several European countries to inspect shipping containers before they are loaded onto ships bound for U.S. shores. Some 11 million such containers enter the country each year, and fewer than 3 percent are inspected for weapons and other contraband.

How will post-9/11 security concerns impinge on free markets and capitalism? What, if any, is the new role of government in such matters? To some, more inspection would seem to be a given. Others say the risk is small and more inspections will only slow commerce and add to cost. In Europe, the European Union has taken legal action against member countries that cut independent inspection deals with the United States. Expect the fight against terror to create more controversy over this key component of capitalism.

Finally, consider a threat to free markets that isn't talked about much—ignorance. As a nation, we aren't as smart as we ought to be, given our wealth and opportunity for education. Collectively, though I hate to say it, we are dumb as posts. As a group, we devote less time to intellectual pursuits than at any time in our history.

We are gathered today in a state that has an 18 percent adult illiteracy rate. Nearly one adult in five can't read well enough to properly fill out a job application. In Michigan's largest city, Detroit, the number is even more devastating. Forty-seven percent of adults are functionally illiterate. How would you like to market a newspaper in that environment? It is hard to convince someone to spend even 50 cents for a product they don't have the skills to use.

The free markets of the future cannot thrive in such a poorly educated society. Higher levels of knowledge and skill will be required of both worker and consumer. The principles of democracy, capitalism, and liberty are not instinctive. They must be taught to each generation.

We discuss the merits of exporting democracy a lot. But democracy in itself is not an answer to anything. We have seen how a democracy can be subverted by an extremist with a populist message. Hitler rose to power in a democratic system.

Democracy must be coupled with education, with knowledge, with an understanding of and commitment to the principles of individual freedom and responsibility, human rights and dignity, and the rule of law. It is essential, then, that the education system in the United States meet its obligation to teach these principles. So far, its record is shameful. The illiteracy rate speaks for itself. In some areas of the country, public education has shortchanged several generations of students and is on track to cheat several generations more.

Industry has long complained of the costs to give new employees basic math and reading training, not to mention instruction in critical thinking and other talents demanded by free markets. In training its employees, businesses are paying for the same service twice: once through the taxes that support public education, and a second time in direct out-of-pocket expenses.

The cost of remedial education has ballooned to a national scandal. Taxpayers cough up an estimated $1 billion a year to teach unprepared college freshmen the basic skills they should have learned in high school. President Bush worries about U.S. colleges becoming institutions of remedial education.

Workable efforts to reform public education are opposed by the public education industry, including teacher unions. Charter schools are one example. In Michigan and elsewhere, charter schools are public schools that operate independently of the public school administration. They are popular with parents, and many individual schools have waiting lists. These schools work on a number of levels, including giving parents direct control over their children's education, and the opportunity to remove their children from failing schools. Yet, in most states, charter schools are either banned or limited. Critics call for pouring more money into traditional education. But the country must ask how much more public money should be put into a system that—even by its own standards—is failing on such a large scale.

We cannot afford to be cavalier about the education of our children. We must insist that every student have the opportunity to learn in a school that works.

Those schools should commit themselves to teaching free market values. There is no room for relativism here. These are the values that form the foundation of American society, and they have been proven superior to any other economic system.

But they will not survive unless the citizenry understands why an open market is better than one controlled by government regulations, how free trade creates jobs, why the marketplace is the best arbiter of supply and demand.

Note

[1]Dr. Robert Cihak, president of the Association of American Physicians and Surgeons, "Health Care Quality: Would It Survive a Single-Payer System?" *Medical Sentinel, 2001,* 6(4): 113–14. ©2001 Association of American Physicians and Surgeons.

LUDWIG VON MISES

The Historical Setting of the Austrian School of Economics

Carl Menger and the Austrian School of Economics

The Beginnings

What is known as the "Austrian School of Economics" started in 1871 when Carl Menger published a slender volume under the title *Grundsätze der Volkswirthschaftslehre*.

It is customary to trace the influence that the milieu exerted upon the achievements of genius. People like to ascribe the exploits of a man of genius, at least to some extent, to the operation of his environment and to the climate of opinion of his age and his country. Whatever this method may accomplish in some cases, there is no doubt that it is inapplicable with regard to those Austrians whose thoughts, ideas, and doctrines matter for mankind. Bernard Bolzano, Gregor Mendel, and Sigmund Freud were not stimulated by their relatives, teachers, colleagues, or friends. Their exertions did not meet with sympathy on the part of their contemporary countrymen and the government of their country. Bolzano and Mendel carried on their main work in surroundings, which, as far as their special fields are concerned, could be called an intellectual desert, and they died long before people began to divine the worth of their contributions. Freud was laughed at when he first made public his doctrines in the Vienna Medical Association.

From *Austrian Economics: An Anthology* (Irvington-on-Hudson, NY: The Foundation for Economic Education, Inc., 1996), pp. 53–76. Originally published by Arlington House (1969). Reprinted with permission.

One may say that the theory of subjectivism and marginalism that Carl Menger developed was in the air. It had been foreshadowed by several forerunners. Besides, about the same time Menger wrote and published his book, William Stanley Jevos and Léon Walras also wrote and published books which expounded the concept of marginal utility. However this may be, it is certain that none of his teachers, friends, or colleagues took any interest in the problems that excited Menger. Some time before the outbreak of the first World War when I told him about the informal but regular meetings in which we younger Vienna economists used to discuss problems of economic theory, he pensively observed: "When I was your age, nobody in Vienna cared about these things." Until the end of the 1870s, there was no "Austrian School." There was only Carl Menger.

Eugene von Böhm-Bawerk and Friedrich von Wieser never studied with Menger. They had finished their studies at the University of Vienna before Menger began to lecture as a *Privatdozent*. What they learned from Menger, they got from studying the *Grundsätze*. When they returned to Austria after some time spent at German universities, especially in the seminar of Karl Knies in Heidelberg, and published their first books, they were appointed to teach economics at the Universities of Innsbruck and Prague, respectively. Very soon some younger men who had gone through Menger's seminar, and had been exposed to his personal influence, enlarged the number of authors who contributed to economic inquiry. People abroad began to refer to these authors as "the Austrians." But the designation "Austrian School of Economics" was used only later, when their antagonism to the German Historical school came into the open after the publication, in 1883, of Menger's second book, *Untersuchungen über die Method der Socialwissenschaften und der Politischen Oekonomie insbesondere.*

The Austrian School of Economics and
the Austrian Universities

The Austrian Cabinet in whose journalistic department Menger served in the early 1870s—before his appointment in 1873 as assistant professor at the University of Vienna—was composed of members of the Liberal Party that stood for civil liberties, representative government, equality of all citizens under the law, sound money, and free trade. At the end of the 1870s the Liberal Party was evicted by an alliance of the Church, the princes and counts of the Czech and Polish aristocracy, and the nationalist parties of the various Slavonic nationalities. This coalition was opposed to all the ideals which the Liberals had supported. However, until the disintegration of the Habsburg Empire in 1918, the Constitution which the Liberals had induced the Emperor to accept in 1867 and the fundamental laws that complemented it remained by and large valid.

In the climate of freedom that these statutes warranted, Vienna became a center of the harbingers of new ways of thinking. From the middle of the sixteenth to the end of the eighteenth century Austria was foreign to the intellectual effort of Europe. Nobody in Vienna—and still less in other parts of the Austrian dominions—cared for the philosophy, literature, and science of Western Europe. When Leibniz and later David Hume visited Vienna, no indigenes were to be found there who would have been interested in their work.[1] With the exception of Bolzano, no Austrian before the second part of the nineteenth century contributed anything of importance to the philosophical or the historical sciences.

But when the Liberals had removed the fetters that had prevented any intellectual effort, when they had abolished censorship and had denounced the concordat, eminent minds began to converge toward Vienna. Some came from Germany—like the philosophers Lorenz von Stein and Rudolf von Jhering—but most of them came from the Austrian provinces; a few were born Viennese. There was no conformity among these leaders, nor among their followers. Brentano, the ex-Dominican, inaugurated a line of thought that finally led to Husserl's phenomenology. Mach was the exponent of a philosophy that resulted in the logical positivism of Schlick, Carnap, and their "Vienna Circle." Breuer, Freud, and Adler interpreted neurotic phenomena in a way radically different from the methods of Krafft-Ebing and Wagner-Jauregg.

The Austrian "Ministry of Worship and Instruction" looked askance upon all these endeavors. Since the early 1880s the Cabinet Minister and the personnel of this department had been chosen from the most reliable conservatives and foes of all modern ideas and political institutions. They had nothing but contempt for what in their eyes were "outlandish fads." They would have liked to bar the universities from access to all this innovation.

But the power of the administration was seriously restricted by three "privileges" which the universities had acquired under the impact of Liberal ideas. The professors were civil servants and, like all other civil servants, bound to obey the orders issued by their superiors, i.e., the Cabinet Minister and his aides. However, these superiors did not have the right to interfere with the content of the doctrines taught in the classes and seminars. In this regard the professors enjoyed the much talked about "academic freedom." Furthermore, the Minister was obliged—although this obligation had never been unambiguously stated—to comply in appointing professors, or to speak more precisely in suggesting to the Emperor the appointment of a professor, with the suggestions made by the faculty concerned. Finally there was the institution of the *Privatdozent*. A doctor who had published a scholarly book could ask the faculty to admit him as a free and private teacher of his discipline. If the faculty decided in favor of the petitioner, the consent of the Minister was still required. In practice this consent was, before the days of the Schuschnigg regime, always given. The duly admitted *Privatdozent* was not, in this capacity, a civil servant. Even if the title of professor was accorded to him, he did not receive any compensation from the government. A few *Privatdozents* could live from their own funds. Most of them worked for their living. Their right to collect the fees by the students who attended their courses was in most cases practically valueless.

The effect of this arrangement of academic affairs was that the councils of the professors enjoyed almost unlimited autonomy in the management of their schools. Economics was taught at the Schools of Law and Social Sciences *(Rechts und staatswissenschaftliche Fakultäten)* of the universities. At most of these universities there were two chairs of economics. If one of these chairs became vacant, a body of lawyers had—with the cooperation at most of one economist—to choose the future incumbent. Thus the decision rested with non-economists. It may be fairly assumed that these professors of law were guided by the best intentions. But they were not economists. They had to choose between two opposed schools of thought, the Austrian school on the one hand, and the allegedly "modern" Historical school as taught at the universities of the German Reich on the other hand. Even if no political and nationalistic prepossessions had disturbed their judgment, they could not help becoming somewhat suspicious of a line of thought which the professors of the universities of the German Reich dubbed specifically Austrian. Never before had any new mode of thinking originated in Austria. The Austrian universities had been sterile until—after the revolution of 1848—they had been reorganized according to the model of the German universities. For people who were not familiar with economics, the predicate "Austrian" as applied to a doctrine carried strong overtones of the dark days of the counter-reformation and of Metternich. To an Austrian intellectual, nothing could appear more disastrous than a relapse of his country into the spiritual inanity of the good old days.

Carl Menger, Wieser, and Böhm-Bawerk had obtained their chairs in Vienna, Prague, and Innsbruck before the *Methodenstreit* had begun to appear in the opinion of the Austrian laymen as a conflict between "modern" science and Austrian "backwardness." Their colleagues had no personal grudge against them. But whenever possible they tried to bring followers of the Historical school from Germany to the Austrian universities. Those whom the world called the "Austrian economists" were, in the Austrian universities, somewhat reluctantly tolerated outsiders.

The Austrian School in the Intellectual Life of Austria

The more distinguished among the French and German universities were, in the great age of liberalism, not merely institutions of learning that provided the rising generations of professional people with the instruction required for the satisfactory practice of their profession. They were centers of culture. Some of their teachers were known and admired all over the world. Their courses were attended not only by the regular students who planned to take academic degrees but by many mature men and women who were active in the professions, business, or politics, and expected from the lectures nothing but intellectual gratification. For instance, such outsiders, who were not students in a technical sense, thronged the courses in Paris of Renan, Fustel de Coulanges, and Bergson, and in Berlin those of Hegel, Helmholtz, Mommsen, and Treitschke. The education public was seriously interested in the work of the academic circles. The elite read the books and the magazines published by the professors, joined their scholastic societies, and eagerly followed the discussions of the meetings.

Some of these amateurs who devoted only leisure hours to their studies rose high above the level of dilettantism. The history of modern science records the names of many such glorious "outsiders." It is, for instance, a characteristic fact that the only remarkable, although not epoch-making, contribution to economics that originated in the Germany of the second Reich came from a busy corporation counsel, Heinrich Oswalt from Frankfurt, a city that at the time his book was written had no university.[2]

In Vienna, also, close association of the university teachers with the cultured public of the city prevailed in the last decades of the nineteenth century and in the beginning of our century. It began to vanish when the old masters died or retired and men of smaller stature got their chairs This was the period in which the rank of the Vienna University, as well as the cultural eminence of the city, was upheld and enlarged by a few of the *Privatdozents*. The outstanding case is that of psychoanalysis. It never got any encouragement from any official institution; it grew and thrived outside the university and its only connection with the bureaucratic hierarchy of learning was the fact that Freud was a *Privatdozent* with the meaningless title of professor.

There was in Vienna, as a heritage of the years in which the founders of the Austrian school had finally earned recognition, a lively interest in problems of economics. This interest enabled the present writer to organize a *Privatseminar* in the 1920s, to start the Economic Association, and to set up the Austrian Institute for Trade Cycle Research, that changed its name to the Austrian Institute for Economic Research.

The *Privatseminar* had no connection whatever with the University or any other institution. Twice a month a group of scholars, among them *Privatdozents*, met in the present writer's office in the Austrian Chamber of Commerce. Most of the participants belonged to the age group that had begun academic studies after the end of the first World War. Some were older. They were united by a burning interest in the whole field of the sciences of human action. In the debates, problems of philosophy, epistemology, economic theory, and the various branches of historical research were treated. The *Privatseminar* was discontinued when, in 1934, the present writer was appointed to the chair of international economic relations at the Graduate Institute of International Studies in Geneva, Switzerland.

With the exception of Richard von Strigl, whose early death put an untimely end to a brilliant scientific career, and Ludwig Bettel-heim-Gabillon, about whom we will have more to say, all the members of the *Privatseminar* found a proper field for the continuation of their work as scholars, authors, and teachers outside of Austria.

In the realm of the spirit, Vienna played an eminent role in the years between the establishment of the Parliament in the early 1860s and the invasion of the Nazis in 1938. The flowering came suddenly after centuries of sterility and apathy. The decay had already begun many years before the Nazis intruded.

In all nations and in all periods of history, intellectual exploits were the work of a few men and were appreciated only by a small elite. The many looked upon these feats with hatred and disdain, at best with indifference. In Austria and in Vienna the elite were especially small, and the hatred of the masses and their leaders especially vitriolic.

Böhm-Bawerk and Wieser as Members of the Austrian Cabinet

The unpopularity of economics is the result of its analysis of the effects of privileges. It is impossible to invalidate the economists' demonstration that all privileges hurt the interests of the rest of the nation or at least of a great part of it, that those victimized will tolerate the existence of such privileges only if privileges are granted to them too, and then, when everybody is privileged, nobody wins but everybody loses on account of the resulting general drop in the productivity of labor.[3] However the warnings of the economists are disregarded by the covetousness of people who are fully aware of their inability to succeed in a competitive market without the aid of special privileges. They are confident that they will get more valuable privileges than other groups or that they will be in a position to prevent, at least for some time, any granting of compensatory privileges to other groups. In their eyes the economist is simply a mischief-maker who wants to upset their plans.

When Menger, Böhm-Bawerk, and Wieser began their scientific careers, they were not concerned with the problems of economic policies and with the rejection of interventionism by Classical economics. They considered it as their vocation to put economic theory on a sound basis and they were ready to dedicate themselves entirely to this cause. Menger heartily disapproved of the interventionist policies that the Austrian government—like almost all governments of the epoch—had adopted. But he did not believe that he could contribute to a return to good policies in any other way than by expounding good economics in his books and articles as well as in his university teaching.

Böhm-Bawerk joined the staff of the Austrian Ministry of Finance in 1890. Twice he served for a short time as Minister of Finance in a caretaker cabinet. From 1900 to 1904 he was Minister of Finance in the cabinet headed by Ernest von Körber. Böhm's principles in the conduct of this office were strict maintenance of the legally fixed gold parity of the currency and a budget balanced without any aid from the central bank. An eminent scholar, Ludwig Bettelheim-Gabillon, planned to publish a comprehensive work analyzing Böhm-Bawerk's activity in the Ministry of France. Unfortunately the Nazis killed the author and destroyed his manuscript.[4]

Weiser was for some time during the first World War Minister of Commerce in the Austrian Cabinet. However, his activity was rather impeded by the far-reaching powers already given before Wieser took office to a functionary of the ministry, Richard Riedl. Virtually only matters of secondary importance were left to the jurisdiction of Wieser himself.

The Conflict with the German Historical School

The German Rejection of Classical Economics

The hostility that the teachings of Classical economic theory encountered on the European continent was primarily caused by political prepossessions. Political economy as developed by several generations of English thinkers, brilliantly expounded by Hume and Adam Smith and perfected by Ricardo, was the most exquisite outcome of the philosophy of the Enlightenment. It was the gist of the liberal doctrine that aimed at the establishment of representative government and equality of all individuals under the law. It was not surprising that it was rejected by all those whose privileges it attacked. This propensity to spurn economics was considerably strengthened in Germany by the rising spirit of nationalism. The narrow-minded repudiation of Western civilization—philosophy, science, political doctrine and institutions, art and literature—which finally resulted in Nazism, originated in a passionate detraction of British political economy.

However, one must not forget that there were also other grounds for this revolt against political economy. This new branch of knowledge raised epistemological and philosophical problems for which the scholars did not find a satisfactory solution. It could not be integrated into the traditional system of epistemology and methodology. The empiricist tendency that dominates Western philosophy suggested considering economics as an experimental science like physics and biology. The very idea that a discipline dealing with "practical" problems like prices and wages could have an epistemological character different from that of other disciplines dealing with practical matters, was beyond the comprehension of the age. But on the other hand, only the most bigoted positivists failed to realize that experiments could not be performed in the field about which economic tries to provide knowledge.

We do not have to deal here with the state of affairs as it developed in the age of the neo-positivism or hyper-positivism of the twentieth century. Today, all over the world, but first of all in the United States, hosts of statisticians are busy in institutes devoted to what people believe is "economic research." They collect figures provided by governments and various business units, rearrange, readjust, and reprint them, compute averages, and draw charts. They surmise that they are thereby "measuring" mankind's "behavior" and that there is no difference worth mentioning between their methods of investigation and those applied in the laboratories of physical, chemical, and biological research. They look with pity and contempt upon those economists who as they say, like the botanists of "antiquity," rely upon "much speculative thinking" instead of upon "experiments."[5] And they are fully convinced that out of their restless exertion there will one day emerge final and complete knowledge that will enable the planning authority of the future to make all people perfectly happy.

But with the economists of the first part of the nineteenth century, the misconstruction of the fundamentals of the sciences of human action did not yet go so far. Their attempts to deal with the epistemological problems of economics resulted, of course, in complete failure. Yet, in retrospect, we may say that this frustration was a necessary step on the way that led toward a more satisfactory solution of the problem. It was John Stuart Mill's abortive treatment of the methods of the moral sciences that unwittingly exposed the futility of all arguments advanced in favor of the empiricist interpretation of the nature of economics.

When Germans began to study the works of British Classical economics, they accepted without any qualms the assumption that economic theory is derived from experience. But this simple explanation could not satisfy those who disagreed with the conclusions which, from the Classical doctrine, had to be inferred for political action. They very soon raised questions: Is not the experience from which the British authors derived their theorems different from the experience which would have faced a German author? Is not British economics defective on account of the fact that the material of experience from which it is distilled was only Great Britain and only Great Britain of the Hanoverian Georges? Is there, after all, such a thing as an economic science valid for all countries, nations, and ages?

It is obvious how these three questions were answered by those who considered economics as an experimental discipline. But such an answer was tantamount to the apodictic negation of economics as such. The Historical school would have been consistent if it had rejected the very idea that such a thing as a science of economics is possible, and if it had scrupulously abstained from making any statements other than reports about what had happened at a definite moment of the past in a definite part of the earth. An anticipation of the effects to be expected from a definite event can be made only on the basis of a theory that claims general validity and not merely validity for what happened in the past in a definite country. The Historical school emphatically denied that there are economic theorems of such a universal validity. But this did not prevent them from recommending or rejecting—in the name of science—various opinions or measures necessarily designed to affect future conditions.

There was, e.g., the Classical doctrine concerning the effects of free trade and protection. The critics did not embark upon the (hopeless) task of discovering some false syllogisms in the chain of Ricardo's reasoning. They merely asserted that "absolute" solutions are not conceivable in such matters. There are historical situations, they said, in which the effects brought about by free trade or protection differ from those described by the "abstract" theory of "armchair" authors. To support their view they referred to various historical precedents. In doing this, they blithely neglected to consider that historical facts, being always the joint result of the operation of a multitude of factors, cannot prove or disprove any theorem.

Thus economics in the second German Reich, as represented by the government-appointed university of professors, degenerated into an unsystematic, poorly assorted collection of various scraps of knowledge borrowed from history, geography, technology, jurisprudence, and party politics, larded with deprecatory remarks about the errors in the "abstractions" of the Classical school. Most of the professors more or less eagerly made propaganda in their writings and in their courses for the policies of the Imperial Government: authoritarian conservatism, Sozialpolitik, protectionism, huge armaments, and aggressive nationalism. It would be unfair to consider this intrusion of politics into the treatment of economics as a specifically German phenomenon. It was ultimately caused by the viciousness of the epistemological interpretation of economic theory, a failing that was not limited to Germany.

A second factor that made nineteenth-century Germany in general and especially the German universities look askance upon British political economy was its preoccupation with wealth and its relation to the utilitarian philosophy.

The then prevalent definitions of political economy described it as the science dealing with the production and distribution of wealth. Such a discipline could be nothing but despicable in the eyes of German professors. The professors thought of themselves as people self-denyingly engaged in the pursuit of pure knowledge and not, like the hosts of banausic money-makers, caring for earthly possessions. The mere mention of such base things as wealth and money was taboo among people boasting of their high culture (*Bildung*). The professors of economics could preserve their standing in the circles of their colleagues only by pointing out that the topic of their studies was not the mean concerns of profit-seeking business but historical research, e.g., about the lofty exploits of the Electors of Brandenburg and Kings of Prussia.

No less serious was the matter of utilitarianism. The utilitarian philosophy was not tolerated at German universities. Of the two outstanding German utilitarians, Ludwig Feuerbach never got any teaching job, while Rudolf von Jhering was a teacher of Roman Law. All the misunderstandings that for more than two thousand years have been advanced against Hedonism and Eudaemonism were rehashed by the professors of *Staatswissenschaften* in their criticisms of the British economists.[6] If nothing else had roused the suspicions of the German scholars, they would have condemned economics for the sole reason that Bentham and the Mills had contributed to it.

The Sterility of Germany in the Field of Economics

The German universities were owned and operated by the various kingdoms and grand duchies that formed the Reich.[7] The professors were civil servants and, as such, had to obey strictly the orders and regulations issued by their superiors, the bureaucrats of the ministries of public instruction. This total and unconditional subordination of the universities and their teachings to the supremacy of the governments was challenged—in vain—by German liberal public opinion when, in 1837, the King of Hanover fired seven professors of the University of Göttingen who protested against the King's breach of the constitution. The governments did not heed the public's reaction. They went on discharging professors with whose political or religious doctrines they did not agree. But after some time they resorted to more subtle and more efficacious methods to make the professors loyal supporters of the official policy. They scrupulously sifted the candidates before appointing them. Only reliable men got the chairs. Thus the question of academic freedom receded into the background. The professors of their own accord taught only what the government permitted them to teach.

The war of 1866 had ended the Prussian constitutional conflict. The King's party—the Conservative party of the Junkers, led by Bismarck—triumphed over the Prussian Progressive party that stood for parliamentary government, and likewise over the democratic groups of southern Germany. In the new political setting, first of the *Norddeut-scher Bund* and, after 1871, of the *Deutsches reich*, there was no room left for the "alien" doctrines of Manchesterism and laissez faire. The victors of Königgrätz and Sedan thought they had nothing to learn from the "nation of shopkeepers"—the British—or from the defeated French.

At the outbreak of the war of 1870, one of the most eminent German scientists, Emil du Bois-Reymond, boasted that the University of Berlin was "the intellectual bodyguard of the House of Hohenzollern." This did not mean very much for the natural sciences, but it had a very clear and precise meaning for the sciences of human action. The incumbents of the chairs of history and of *Staatswissenschaften* (i.e., political science, including all things referring to economics and finance) knew what their sovereign expected of them. And they delivered the goods.

From 1882 to 1907 Friedrich Althoff was in the Prussian ministry of instruction in charge of university affairs. He ruled the Prussian universities as a dictator. As Prussia had the greatest number of lucrative professorships, and therefore offered the most favorable field for ambitious scholars, the professors in the other German states, nay even those of Austria and Switzerland, aspired to secure positions in Prussia. Thus Althoff could as a rule make them, too, virtually accept his principles and opinions. In all matters pertaining to the social sciences and the historical disciplines, Althoff entirely relied upon the advice of his friend Gustav von Schmoller. Schmoller had an unerring flair for separating the sheep from the goats.

In the second and third quarters of the nineteenth century some German professors wrote valuable contributions to economic theory. It is true that the most remarkable contributions of this period, those of Thünen and of Gossen, were not the work of professors but of men who did not hold teaching jobs. However, the books of Professors Hermann, Mangoldt, and Knies will be remembered in the history of economic thought. But after 1866, the men who came into the academic career had only contempt for "bloodless abstractions." They published historical studies, preferably such as dealt with labor conditions of the most recent past. Many of them were firmly convinced that the foremost task of economists was to aid the "people in the war of liberation they were waging against the exploiters," and

that the God-given leaders of the people were the dynasties, especially the Hohenzollern.

The *Methodenstreit*

In the *Untersuchungen* Menger rejected the epistemological ideas that
underlay the writings of the Historical school. Schmoller published a
rather contemptuous review of this book. Menger reacted, in 1884,
with a pamphlet, *Die Irrtümer des Historismus in der Deutschen Nation-
alökonomie [The Errors of Historicism in German Economics]*. The various
publications that this controversy engendered are known under the
name of the *Methodenstreit*, the clash over methods.

The *Methodenstreit* contributed but little to the clarification of the
problems involved. Menger was too much under the sway of John Stuart Mill's empiricism to carry his own point of view to its full logical
consequences. Schmoller and his disciples, committed to defend an
untenable position, did not even realize what the controversy was about.

The term *Methodenstreit* is, of course, misleading. For the issue
was not to discover the most appropriate procedure for the treatment
of the problems commonly considered as economic problems. The
matter in dispute was essentially whether there could be such a thing
as a science, other than history, dealing with aspects of human action.

There was, first of all, radical materialist determinism, a philosophy almost universally accepted in Germany at that time by physicists, chemists, and biologists, although it has never been expressly
and clearly formulated. As these people saw it, human ideas, voli-
tions, and actions are produced by physical and chemical events that
the natural sciences will one day describe in the same way in which
today they describe the emergence of a chemical compound out of
the combination of several ingredients. As the only road that could
lead to this final scientific accomplishment they advocated experimentation in physiological and biological laboratories.

Schmoller and his disciples passionately rejected this philosophy, not because they were aware of its deficiencies, but because it
was incompatible with the religious tenets of the Prussian government. They virtually preferred to it a doctrine that was but little different from Comte's positivism, which, of course, they publicly
disparaged on account of its atheism and its French origin. In fact,

positivism, sensibly interpreted, must result in materialist determinism. But most of Comte's followers were not outspoken in this regard. Their discussions did not always preclude the conclusion that the laws of social physics (sociology), the establishment of which was in their opinion the highest goal of science, could be discovered by what they called a more "scientific" method of dealing with the material assembled by the traditional procedures of the historians. This was the position Schmoller embraced with regard to economics. Again and again he blamed the economists for having prematurely made inferences from quantitatively insufficient material. In his opinion, what was needed in order to substitute a realistic science of economics for the hasty generalizations of the British "armchair" economists was more statistics, more history, and more collection of "material." Out of the results of such research the economists of the future, he maintained, would one day develop new insights by "induction."

Schmoller was so confused that he failed to see the incompatibility of his own epistemological doctrine and the rejection of positivism's attack upon history. He did not realize the gulf that separated his views from those of the German philosophers who demolished positivism's ideas about the use and the treatment of history—first Dilthey, and later Windelband, Rickert, and Max Weber. In the same article in which he censured Menger's *Grundsätze*, he reviewed also the first important book of Dilthey, his *Einleitung in die Geisteswissenschaften*. But he did not grasp the fact that the tenor of Dilthey's doctrine was the annihilation of the fundamental thesis of his own epistemology, viz., that some laws of social development could be distilled from historical experience.

The Political Aspects of the *Methodenstreit*

The British free trade philosophy triumphed in the nineteenth century in the countries of western and central Europe. It demolished the shaky ideology of the authoritarian welfare state (*landesfürstlicher Wohlfahrtsstaat*) that had guided the policies of the German principalities in the eighteenth century. The culmination points of its free trade were the *Zollverein*'s customs tariff of 1865 and the 1869 Trade Code (*Gewerbeordnung*) for the territory of the *Norddeutscher Bund* (later the *Deutsches Reich*). But very soon the government of Bismarck began to inaugurate its *Sozialpolitik*, the system of interventionist measures such as labor legislation, social security, pro-union attitudes, progressive taxation, protective tariffs, cartels, and dumping.[8]

If one tries to refute the devastating criticism leveled by economics against the suitability of all these interventionist schemes, one is forced to deny the very existence—not to mention the epistemological claims—of a science of economics, and of praxeology as well. This is what all the champions of authoritarianism, government omnipotence, and "welfare" policies have always done. They blame economics for being "abstract" and advocate a "visualizing" (*anschaulich*) mode of dealing with the problems involved. They emphasize that matters in this field are too complicated to be described in formulas and theorems. They assert that the various nations and races are so different from one another that their actions cannot be comprehended by a uniform theory; there are as many economic theories required as there are nations and races. Others add that even within the same nation or race, economic action is different in various epochs of history. These and similar objections, often incompatible with one another, are advanced in order to discredit economics as such.

In fact, economics disappeared entirely from the universities of the German Empire. There was a lone epigone of Classical economics left at the University of Bonn, Heinrich Dietzel, who, however, never understood what the theory of subjective value meant. At all other universities the teachers were anxious to ridicule economics and the economists. It is not worthwhile to dwell upon the stuff that was handed down as a substitute for economics at Berlin, Munich, and other universities of the Reich. Nobody cares today about all that Gustav von Schmoller, Adolph Wagner, Lujo Brentano, and their numerous adepts wrote in their voluminous books and magazines.

The political significance of the work of the Historical school consisted in the fact that it rendered Germany safe for the ideas, the acceptance of which made popular with the German people all those disastrous policies that resulted in the great catastrophes. The aggressive imperialism that twice ended in war and defeat, the limitless inflation of the early 1920s, the *Zwangswirtschaft* [command economy] and all the horrors of the Nazi regime were achievements of politicians who acted as they had been taught by the champions of the Historical school.

Schmoller and his friends and disciples advocated what has been called state socialism; i.e., a system of socialism—planning—in which the top management would be in the hands of the Junker aristocracy. It was this brand of socialism at which BIsmarck and his successors were aiming. The timid opposition which they encountered on the part of a small group of businessmen was negligible, not so much on account of the fact that these opponents were not numerous, but because their endeavors lacked any ideological backing. There were no longer any liberal thinkers left in Germany. The only resistance that was offered to the party of state socialism came from the Marxian party of the Social-Democrats. Like the Schmoller socialists—the socialists of the chair (*Kathedersozialisten*)—the Marxists advocated socialism. The only difference between the two groups was in the choice of the people who should operate the supreme planning board: the Junkers, the professors, and the bureaucracy of Hohenzollern Prussia, or the offices of the Social-Democratic party and their affiliated labor unions.

Thus the only serious adversaries whom the Schmoller school had to fight in Germany were the Marxists. In this controversy the latter very soon got the upper hand. For they at least had a body of doctrine, however faulty and contradictory it was, while the teachings of the Historical school were rather the denial of any theory. In search of a modicum of theoretical support, the Schmoller school step by step began to borrow from the spiritual fund of the Marxists. Finally, Schmoller himself largely endorsed the Marxian doctrine of class conflict and of the "ideological" impregnation of thought by the thinker's class membership. One of his friends and fellow professors, Wilhelm Lexis, developed a theory of interest that Engels characterized as a paraphrase of the Marxian theory of exploitation.[9] It was an effect of the writings of the champions of the *Sozialpolitik* that the epithet "bourgeois" (*Bürgerlich*) acquired in the German language an opprobrious connotation.

The crushing defeat in the first World War shattered the prestige of the German princes, aristocrats, and bureaucrats. The adepts of the Historical school and *Sozialpolitik* transferred their loyalty to various splinter-groups, out of which the German National-Socialist Workers' Party, the Nazis, eventually emerged.

The straight line that leads from the work of the Historical school to Nazism cannot be shown in sketching the evolution of one of the founders of the school, for the protagonists of the *Methodenstreit* era had finished the course of their lives before the defeat of 1918 and the rise of Hitler. But the life of the outstanding man among the school's second generation illustrates all the phases of German university economics in the period from Bismarck to Hitler.

Werner Sombart was by far the most gifted of Schmoller's students. He was only twenty-five when his master, at the height of the M*ethodenstreit*, entrusted him with the job of reviewing and annihilating Wieser's book, *Der natürliche Wert*. The faithful disciple condemned the book as "entirely unsound."[10] Twenty years later Sombart boasted that he had dedicated a good part of his life to fighting for Marx.[11] When the War broke out in 1914, Sombart published a book, *Händler und Helden [Hucksters and Heroes]*.[12] There, in uncouth and foul language, he rejected everything British or Anglo-Saxon, but above all British philosophy and economics, as a manifestation of a mean jobber mentality. After the War, Sombart revised his book on socialism. Before the War it had been published in nine editions.[13] While the pre-war editions had praised Marxism, the tenth edition fanatically attacked it, especially on account of its "proletarian" character and its lack of patriotism and nationalism. A few years later Sombart tried to revive the *Methodenstreit* by a volume full of invectives against economists whose thought he was unable to understand.[14] Then when the Nazis seized power, he crowned a literary career of forty-five years by a book on German Socialism. The guiding idea of this work was that the *Führer* gets his orders from God, the supreme *Führer* of the universe, and that *Führertum* is a permanent revelation.[15]

Such was the progress of German academic economics from Schmoller's glorification of the Hohenzollern Electors and Kings to Sombart's canonization of Adolf Hitler.

The Liberalism of the Austrian Economists

Plato dreamed of the benevolent tyrant who would entrust the wise philosopher with the power to establish the perfect social system. The Enlightenment did not put its hopes upon the more or less accidental emergence of well-intentioned rulers and provident sages. Its optimism concerning mankind's future was founded upon the double faith in the goodness of man and in his rational mind. In the past a minority of villains—crooked kings, sacrilegious priests, corrupt noblemen—were able to make mischief. But now—according to Enlightenment doctrine—as man has become aware of the power of his reason, a relapse into the darkness and failings of ages gone by is no longer to be feared. Every new generation will add something to the good accomplished by its ancestors. Thus mankind is on the eve of a continuous advance toward more satisfactory conditions. To progress steadily is the nature of man. It is vain to complain about the alleged lost bliss of a fabulous golden age. The ideal state of society is before us, not behind us.

Most of the nineteenth-century liberal, progressive, and democratic politicians who advocated representative government and universal suffrage were guided by a firm confidence in the infallibility of the common man's rational mind. In their eyes majorities could not err. Ideas that originated from the people and were approved by the voters could not but be beneficial to the commonweal.

It is important to realize that the arguments brought forward in favor of representative government by the small group of liberal philosophers were quite different and did not imply any reference to an alleged infallibility of majorities. Hume had pointed out that government is always founded upon opinion. In the long run the opinion of the many always wins out. A government that is not supported by the opinion of the majority must sooner or later lose its power; if it does not abdicate, it is violently overthrown by the many. Peoples have the power eventually to put those men at the helm who are prepared to rule according to the principles that the majority considers adequate. There is, in the long run, no such thing as an unpopular government maintaining a system that the multitude condemns as unfair. The rationale of representative government is not that majorities are Godlike and infallible; it is the intent to bring about by peaceful methods the ultimately unavoidable adjustment of the political system and the men operating its steering mechanism to the ideology of the majority. The horrors of revolution and civil war can be avoided if a disliked government can be smoothly dislodged at the next election.

The true liberals firmly held that the market economy, the only economic system that warrants a steadily progressing improvement of mankind's material welfare, can work only in an atmosphere of undisturbed peace. They advocated government by the people's elected representatives because they took it for granted that only this system will lastingly preserve peace both in domestic and in foreign affairs.

What separated these true liberals from the blind majority-worship of the self-styled radicals was that they based their optimism concerning mankind's future not upon the mystic confidence in the infallibility of majorities but upon the belief that the power of sound logical argument is irresistible. They did not fail to see that the immense majority of common men are both too dull and too indolent to follow and to absorb long chains of reasoning. But they hoped that these masses, precisely on account of their dullness and indolence, could not help endorsing the ideas that the intellectuals brought to them. From the sound judgment of the cultured minority and from their ability to persuade the majority, the great leaders of the nineteenth-century liberal movement expected the steady improvement of human affairs.

In this regard there was full agreement between Carl Menger and his two earliest followers, Wieser and Böhm-Bawerk. Among the unpublished papers of Menger, Professor Hayek discovered a note that reads: "There is no better means to disclose the absurdity of a mode of reasoning than to let it pursue its full course to the end." All three of them liked to refer to Spinoza's argumentation in the first book of his *Ethics* that ends in the famous dictum, "*Sane sicut lux se ipsam et tenebras manifestat, sic veritas norma sui et falsi"]* ["Indeed, just as light defines itself and darkness, so truth sets the standard for itself and falsity"]. They looked calmly upon the passionate propaganda of both the Historical school and Marxism. They were fully convinced that the logically indefensible dogmas of these factions would eventually be rejected by all reasonable men precisely on account of their absurdity and that the masses of common men would necessarily follow the lead of the intellectuals.[16]

The wisdom of this mode of arguing is to be seen in the avoidance of the popular practice of playing off an alleged psychology against logical reasoning. It is true that often errors in reasoning are caused by the individual's disposition to prefer an erroneous conclusion to the correct one. There are even hosts of people whose affec-

tions simply prevent them from straight thinking. But it is a far cry
from the establishment of these facts to the doctrines that in the last
generation were taught under the label "sociology of knowledge."
Human thinking and reasoning, human science and technology are
the product of a social process insofar as the individual thinker faces
both the achievements and the errors of his predecessors and enters
into a virtual discussion with them either in assenting or dissenting.
It is possible for the history of ideas to make understandable a man's
failings as well as his exploits by analyzing the conditions under which
he lived and worked. In this sense only is it permissible to refer to
what is called the spirit of an age, a nation, a milieu. But it is circular
reasoning if one tries to explain the emergence of an idea, still less to
justify it, by referring to its author's environment. Ideas always spring
from the mind of an individual, and history cannot say anything more
about them than that they were generated at a definite instant of
time by a definite individual. There is no other excuse for a man's
erroneous thinking than what an Austrian government once declared
with regard to the case of a defeated general—that nobody is answer-
able for not being a genius. Psychology may help us to explain why a
man failed in his thinking. But no such explanation can convert what
is false into truth.

The Austrian economists unconditionally rejected the logical
relativism implied in the teachings of the Prussian or German Historical school. As against the declarations of Schmoller and his followers, they maintained that there is a body of economic theorems that
are valid for all human action irrespective of time and place, the national and racial characteristics of the actors, and their religious, philosophical, and ethical ideologies.

The greatness of the service these three Austrian economists
have rendered by maintaining the cause of economics against the
vain critique of Historicism cannot be overrated. They did not infer
from their epistemological convictions any optimism concerning mankind's future evolution. Whatever is to be said in favor of correct logical thinking does not prove that the coming generations of men will
surpass their ancestors in intellectual effort and achievements. History shows that again and again periods of marvelous mental accomplishments were followed by periods of decay and retrogression. We

do not know whether the next generation will beget people who are able to continue along the lines of the geniuses who made the last centuries so glorious. We do not know anything about the biological conditions that enable a man to make one step forward in the march of intellectual advancement. We cannot preclude the assumption that there may be limits to man's further intellectual ascent. And certainly we do not know whether in this ascent there is not a point beyond which the intellectual leaders can no longer succeed in convincing the masses and making them follow their lead.

The inference drawn from these premises by the Austrian economists was that, while it is the duty of a pioneering mind to do all that his faculties enable him to perform, it is not incumbent upon him to propagandize for his ideas, still less to use questionable methods in order to make his thoughts palatable to people. They were not concerned about the circulation of their writings. Menger did not publish a second edition of his famous *Grundsätze*, although the book was long since out of print, second-hand copies sold at high prices, and the publisher urged him again and again to consent.

The main and only concern of the Austrian economists was to contribute to the advancement of economics. They never tried to win the support of anybody by other means than by the convincing power developed in their books and articles. They looked with indifference upon the fact that the universities of the German-speaking countries, even many of the Austrian universities, were hostile to economics as such and still more so to the new economic doctrines of subjectivism.

The Place of the Austrian School of Economics in the Evolution of Economics

The "Austrian School" and Austria

When the German professors attached the epithet "Austrian" to the theories of Menger and his two earliest followers and continuators, they meant it in a pejorative sense. After the battle of Königgrätz — 1866, when the Prussians under William I roundly defeated the Austrian army—the qualification of a thing as Austrian always had such a derogatory coloration in Berlin, that "headquarters of *Geist*" as Her-

bert Spencer sneeringly called it.[17] But the intended smear boomer-
anged. Very soon the designation "The Austrian School" was famous
all over the world.

Of course, the practice of attaching a national label to a line of
thought is necessarily misleading. Only very few Austrians—and for
that matter, non-Austrians—knew anything about economics, and still
smaller was the number of those Austrians whom one could call economists, however generous one might be in conferring this appellation. Besides, there were among the Austrian-born economists some
who did not work along the lines which were called the "Austrian
School." Best known among them were the mathematicians Rudolf
Auspitz and Richard Lieben, and later Alfred Amonn and Josef Schumpeter. On the other hand, the number of foreign economists who applied themselves to the continuation of the work inaugurated by the
"Austrians" was steadily increasing. At the beginning it sometimes happened that the endeavors of these British, American, and other non-
Austrian economists met with opposition in their own countries and
that they were ironically called "Austrians" by their critics. But after
some years all the essential ideas of the Austrian school were by and
large accepted as an integral part of economic theory. About the time
of Menger's demise (1921), one no longer distinguished between an
Austrian school and other economics. The appellation "Austrian
School" became the name given to an important chapter of the history of economic thought; it was no longer the name of a specific sect
with doctrines different from those held by other economists.

There was, of course, one exception. The interpretation of the
causes and the course of the trade cycle which the present writer provided, first in his *Theory of Money and Credit*[18] and finally in his treatise
Human Action[19] under the name of the Monetary or Circulation Credit
Theory of the trade cycle, was called by some authors the Austrian
theory of the trade cycle. Like all such national labels, this too is ob-
jectionable. The Circulation Credit Theory is a continuation, enlarge-
ment, and generalization of ideas first developed by the British
Currency School and of some additions to them made by later economists, among them also the Swede, Knut Wicksell.

As it has been unavoidable to refer to the national label, "the
Austrian School," one may add a few words about the linguistic group

to which the Austrian economists belonged. Menger, Böhm-Bawerk, and Wieser were German Austrians; their language was German and they wrote their books in German. The same is true of their most eminent students—Johann von Komorzynski, Hans Mayer, Robert Meyer, Richard Schüller, Richard von Strigl, and Robert Zuckerkandl. In this sense the work of the Austrian school is an accomplishment of German philosophy and science. But among the students of Menger, Böhm-Bawerk, and Wieser there were also non-German Austrians. Two of them have distinguished themselves by eminent contributions, the Czechs Franz Cuhel and Karel Englis.

The Historical Significance of the *Methodenstreit*

The peculiar state of German ideological and political conditions in the last quarter of the nineteenth century generated the conflict between two schools of thought out of which the *Methodenstreit* and the appellation "Austrian School" emerged. But the antagonism that manifested itself in this debate is not confined to a definite period or country. It is perennial. As human nature is, it is unavoidable in any society where the division of labor and its corollary, market exchange, have reached such an intensity that everybody's subsistence depends on other people's conduct. In such a society everybody is served by his fellow men, and in turn, he serves them. The services are rendered voluntarily: in order to make a fellow do something for me, I have to offer him something which he prefers to abstention from doing that something. The whole system is built upon this voluntariness of the services exchanged. Inexorable natural conditions prevent man from indulging in a carefree enjoyment of his existence. But his integration into the community of the market economy is spontaneous, the result of the insight that there is no better or, for that matter, no other method of survival open to him.

However, the meaning and bearing of this spontaneousness are only grasped by economists. All those not familiar with economics, i.e., the immense majority, do not see any reason why they should not coerce other people by means of force to do what these people are not prepared to do of their own accord. Whether this apparatus of physical compulsion resorted to in such endeavors is that of the government's police power or an illegal "picket" force whose violence the government tolerates, does not make any difference. What matters is the substitution of compulsion for voluntary action.

Due to a definite constellation of political conditions that could be called accidental, the rejection of the philosophy of peaceful cooperation was, in modern times, first developed into a comprehensive doctrine by subjects of the Prussian State. The victories in the three Bismarck wars had intoxicated the German scholars, most of whom were servants of the government. Some people considered it a characteristic fact that the adoption of the ideas of the Schmoller school was slowest in the countries whose armies had been defeated in 1866 and 1870. It is, of course, preposterous to search for any connection between the rise of the Austrian economic theory and the defeats, failures, and frustrations of the Habsburg regime. Yet, the fact that the French state universities kept out of the way of historicism and *Sozialpolitik* longer than those of other nations was certainly, at least to some extent, caused by the Prussian label attached to these doctrines. France, like all other countries, became a stronghold of interventionism and proscribed economics.

The philosophical consummation of the ideas glorifying the government's interference, i.e., the action of the armed constables, was achieved by Nietzsche and by Georges Sorel. They coined most of the slogans that guided the butcheries of Bolshevism, Fascism, and Nazism. Intellectuals extolling the delights of murder, writers advocating censorship, philosophers judging the merits of thinkers and authors, not according to the value of their contributions but according to their achievements on battlefields,[20] are spiritual leaders of our age of perpetual strife. What a spectacle was offered by those American authors and professors who ascribed the origin of their own nation's political independence and constitution to a clever trick of the "special interests," while casting longing glances at the Soviet paradise of Russia!

The greatness of the nineteenth century consisted in the fact that to some extent the ideas of Classical economics became the dominant philosophy of state and society. They transformed the traditional status society into nations of free citizens, royal absolutism into representative government, and above all, the poverty of the masses under the *ancien régime* into the well-being of the many under capitalistic laissez faire. Today the reaction of statism and socialism is sapping the foundations of Western civilization and well-being. Perhaps those are right who assert that it is too late to prevent the final triumph of barbarism and destruction. However this may be, one thing is certain—society, i.e., peaceful cooperation of men under the principle of the division of labor, can exist and work only if it adopts policies that economic analysis declares as fit for attaining the ends sought. The worst illusion of our age is the superstitious confidence placed in panaceas which—as the economists have irrefutably demonstrated—are contrary to purpose.

Governments, political parties, pressure groups, and the bureaucrats of the educational hierarchy think they can avoid the inevitable consequences of unsuitable measures by boycotting and silencing the independent economists. But truth persists and works, even if nobody is left to utter it.

Notes

[1] The only contemporary Viennese who appreciated the philosophic work of Leibniz was Prince Eugene of Savoy, scion of a French family, born and educated in France.

[2] *Cf.* H. Oswalt, *Vortäge über wirtschaftliche Grundbegriffe*, 3rd ed. (Jena, 1920).

[3] Cf. Mises, *Human Action* (1949) and later editions, chapters XXVII–XXXVI.

[4] Only two chapters, which the author had published before the Anschluss, are preserved: "Böhm-Bawerk und die Brüsseler Zuckerkonvention" and "Böhm-Bawerk und die Konvertierung von Obligationen der einheitlichen Staatsschuld" in *Zeitschrift fur Nationalökomie*, Vol. VII and VIII (1936 and 1937).

[5] *Cf.* Arthur F. Burns, *The Frontiers of Economic Knowledge* (Princeton University Press, 1954), p. 189.

[6] Later similar arguments were employed to discredit pragmatism. William James's dictum according to which the pragmatic method aims at bringing out of each word "its practical cash-value" (*Pragmatism*, 1907, p. 53) was quoted to characterize the meanness of the "dollar-philosophy."

[7] The Reich itself owned and operated only the University of Strassburg. The three German city-republics did not at that period have any university.

[8] *Cf.* Mises, *Omnipotent Government* (Yale University Press, 1944, and later editions), pp. 149ff.

[9] *Cf.* the more detailed analysis in Mises, *Kritik des Interventionismus* (Jena, 1929), pp. 92ff. [English translation: *Critique of Interventionism* (Arlington House, 1977), pp. 108ff.]

[10]Cf. *Schmoller's Jahrbuch*, Vol. 13 (1889), pp. 1488–1490.

[11]*Cf.* Sombart, *Das Lebenswerk von Karl Marx* (Jena, 1909), p. 3

[12]*Cf.* Sombart, *Händler und Helden* (Munich, 1915).

[13]*Cf.* Sombart, *Der proletarische Sozialismus*, 10th ed. (Jena, 1924), 2 vol.

[14]*Cf.* Sombart, *Die drei nationalökonmien* (Munich, 1930).

[15]*Cf.* Sombart, *Deutscher Sozialismus* (Charlottenburg, 1934), p. 213. (In the American edition: *A New Social Philosophy*, translated and edited by K. F. Geiser, Princeton, 1937, p. 149.) Sombart's achievements were appreciated abroad. Thus, e.g., in 1929 he was elected to honorary membership in the American Economic Association.

[16]There is need to add that Menger, Böhm-Bawerk, and Wieser looked with the utmost pessimism upon the political future of the Austrian Empire. But this problem cannot be dealt with in this essay.

[17]*Cf.* Herbert Spencer, *The Study of Sociology*, 9th edition (London, 1880), p. 217.

[18] German-language editions, 1912 and 1924, English-language editions 1934, 1953 [1980].

[19]First edition, Yale University Press, 1949; 4th edition, Foundation for Economic Education, 1996.

[20]*Cf.* the passages quoted by Julien Brenda, *La trahison des clercs* (Paris, 1927), Appendix, Note O, pp. 292–295 [English translation, *The Betrayal of the Intellectuals*, Boston: Beacon Press, 155. ed.].